FIVE HUNDRED QUESTIONS KIDS ASK ABOUT SEX

And Some of the Answers

ABOUT THE AUTHOR

Frances Younger grew up and graduated from high school in the mid-Michigan city of Lansing. She attended both Stephens Junior College for Women and Oberlin College, graduating in 1942.

In 1942, she married a young attorney, Paul Younger, and accompanied him to several military posts where he was assigned duty. Settled in Lansing after the war, she became a homemaker for their three children, part-time vocal teacher and assistant to her husband in his political campaigns. Over the next fifteen years, he was judge, prosecuting attorney, and state senator.

In 1968, she graduated from Michigan State University with a master's degree in secondary counseling. She accepted a position as teacher in growth and development (sex education) with an area school district and continued in this position until her retirement in 1983.

In 1977, she was elected a member of the American Association of Sex Educators, Counselors and Therapists (AASECT). For several years, she taught parenting classes for the adult night school and Lansing Community College. At the community college, she developed and taught classes in Female Sexuality and in social skills and sexuality for the adult handicapped.

She is presently assistant for workshops sponsored by Michigan State University and Ingham Intermediate School District. These workshops are approved and required by the state of Michigan, for all teachers who are assigned or are teaching sex education in their own district.

FIVE HUNDRED QUESTIONS KIDS ASK ABOUT SEX

And Some of the Answers

Sex Education for Parents, Teachers and Young People Themselves

By

FRANCES YOUNGER, M.A.

CHARLES C THOMAS • PUBLISHER

Springfield • Illinois • U.S.A.

Published and Distributed Throughout the World by

CHARLES C THOMAS • PUBLISHER
2600 South First Street
Springfield, Illinois 62794-9265

© *1992 by* CHARLES C THOMAS • PUBLISHER
ISBN 0-398-05789-3 (cloth)
ISBN 0-398-06509-8 (paper)
Library of Congress Catalog Card Number: 91-47078

With THOMAS BOOKS *careful attention is given to all details of manufacturing
and design. It is the Publisher's desire to present books that are satisfactory as to
their physical qualities and artistic possibilities and appropriate for their particular
use.* THOMAS BOOKS *will be true to those laws of quality that assure a good
name and good will.*

Printed in the United States of America
SC-R-3

Library of Congress Cataloging-in-Publication Data

Younger, Frances.
 Five hundred questions kids ask about sex : and some of the
answers / by Frances Younger.
  p.   cm.
 Includes bibliographical references and index.
 ISBN 0-398-05789-3. — ISBN 0-398-06509-8 (pbk.)
  1. Sex instruction.   2. Sex instruction for children.   3. Sex
instruction for youth.   I. Title.
HQ57.3.Y68   1992
649'.65 — dc20
                                                              91-47078
                                                                 CIP

ACKNOWLEDGEMENTS

This book was made possible by the participation of hundreds of students. They took part in many lively discussions about sex and seemed to appreciate being given "straight answers" to their many questions.

I want to thank all of the classroom teachers who allowed the "sex education lady" to come into their classes to teach this program. Their active support made it much more productive.

No sex education teacher can "know it all." A special thank you goes to the many specialists from the medical and public health fields in the area. Many gave generously of their time and expertise. A special thank-you goes to Mary McCartney, assistant professor at Michigan State University's College of Nursing and a personal friend. She gave me much encouragement and information over the many years we worked together. She reviewed several sections of this book, adding accuracy and information to much of it.

Also helping with the review of this book were Susan MacArthur, a nurse at a teen clinic, and Larry Keyes from the county veneral disease or sexually transmitted disease clinic.

I wish to give a special thank-you to Michael Monheit, a teacher at Michigan State University. He patiently reviewed and rewrote the script to make it more readable. He added his own unique viewpoint to the book and yet kept the original information and spirit as well. I also want to thank Carey Draeger for her skillful help and preparation of this manuscript.

INTRODUCTION

"What kinds of questions about sex do kids ask?" "How would you answer a question like that?" When the subject of sex education comes up, these are the two most frequently asked questions which parents, teachers and others concerned with sex education ask.

This book is designed for parents, teachers and young people themselves. It is based on the premise that sexual expression is a wonderful way that people can show affection and love for each other, despite the many conflicts and problems it may cause for the young and not-so-young. I think it will be especially useful for those people who desire to talk frankly to children and teenagers in their care, but are still hesitant and embarrassed because they themselves have not experienced straightforward and frank discussions of sexual information. Although other valuable books on sex education are available which advocate frankness and honesty, mine provides parents and teachers with examples of precise and no-holds-barred responses their children will understand.

This book is based on fifteen years of experience in teaching young people about sex, in training sex education teachers, in raising three children and in caring for three grandchildren. Out of my own experience, and in consultation with many colleagues and friends, I have reviewed close to 2,500 actual questions asked by children and teenagers from kindergarten through high school and selected those questions which young people most frequently ask.

Some people may question the need for frank discussions of sex with young people, given how often sex is openly portrayed in the mass media. Yet, although often very explicit, most depictions of sex are very unrealistic and suggest that sex has no consequences beyond the pleasure and romance of the moment. Rarely do popular portrayals suggest that there might be more to sexual feelings than intense physical attraction. They almost always lack any sense of responsibility. Television and films often arouse and exploit our young people's sexual impulses with little regard for the resulting teen pregnancies, unwanted children or deeply hurt feelings.

To be sure, the so-called "sexual revolution" has made it easier for us to speak openly and frankly about sex. Nevertheless, the impact of this "revolution" is much overrated. Over the years, I have seen how poorly informed about sex young people are. At the beginning of the 1990s young people ask the same questions that they did in 1967, and reveal the same confusion and misinformation. What has changed is that now they ask more "advanced" questions at younger ages.

Unfortunately, what has not changed enough is our willingness as adults to provide honest responses and correct information to our children. Strong sexual feelings are a daily reality for young people, as any adult who thinks back to her or his teen years will remember. Yet so often parents and teachers try to pretend that they don't exist or that they pose no difficult problems for our children. Perhaps this is because our own youthful sexual feelings were troubling, associated with anxieties we would just as soon forget. Because of the reluctance of mature adults, I have seen countless young people seriously damage their potential for happiness and success. Sometimes they have not learned how to control these feelings, but frequently they are simply misinformed about the basic facts of how a woman becomes pregnant and how pregnancy may be avoided. Because parents, teachers, counsellors and ministers are often unwilling or uncomfortable to discuss sex in a frank and honest manner, our children fill in the vacuum with highly distorted pictures of sex derived from television and films.

Whether we like it or not, our young people today will learn about sex at a young age. It is up to us to see to it that they do not learn from the mass media that sex involves no responsibility, can be enjoyed fully without any commitment or emotional involvement, and has no consequences. One of the most difficult problems is to respond to the whole person's concerns, not just to the realities of his or her sexual desire. It is often easier to give technical information about sexual activity and sexual development than it is to respond clearly to the complex ways that sexual feelings are involved with other feelings—the desire for emotional intimacy with a member of the opposite sex, the wish to impress one's friends and to "belong," the struggle for independence from one's elders. Ultimately, these are all issues each young person must work out for himself or herself. I have found that young teenagers act responsibly, if we acknowledge the reality and power of their feelings and if we show them our confidence in their ability and desire to understand and take charge of their feelings and express them responsibly. It is very normal for teenagers to want to experiment: to hug, to kiss, to stroke each other's sexual areas and to have sexual intercourse. It is my deepest conviction that by acknowledging and discussing these desires openly, adults are able to help teenagers engage in responsible sex in which the partners treat each other with respect. It is our very **unwillingness** to be forthright that leaves our young people feeling pressured to have sexual intercourse in order to impress their friends or appear "grown-up," to pretend they already know all there is to know about sex.

I have set down the questions in much the same form that pre-teens and teenagers ask them, and provided clear, unambiguous and comprehensive answers to each. I have kept the slang or "street" terms in the questions because—like it or not—these are the words youngsters most easily understand. One of my colleagues relishes an incident in which a child, well schooled in the polite, technical language of sex, asked, "I know all about the penis, the vagina, the testicles and the ovaries; but what does my dickie do?" Youngsters have heard the slang terms for years, and are usually more comfortable using them than the correct terms. By not reacting with shock or disapproval to a youngster's use of such terms, you will make it easier to establish trust with her or him. In my answers, I try to lead the youngster to learn and use the more correct terminology. I have found that after continual repetition, the youngsters themselves begin to prefer them to "street" language. I have tried to keep repetition to a minimum. But some repetition is necessary, both to reinforce the young person's knowledge and to enable him or her to connect one piece of information with another.

In answering questions it is important to remember that questions may express not only a young person's curiosity, but also his or her anxiety as well. Many spoken questions often contain the unspoken questions, "Am I normal?" "Is this normal?" Someone might ask merely out of curiosity, "What decides if a baby will be a boy or a girl?" On the other hand, someone may ask because of anxiety, "Will you die from masturbating?" Sometimes a question may appear to merely express curiosity, while in reality the young person is seeking to put to rest some anxiety. One example might be, "At what age to boys (or girls) begin to mature sexually?" The person may seem merely to be curious, but in reality is wondering whether he or she has something wrong with him or her because sexual development has not yet begun. The question "Can you tell a homosexual by his or her looks?" can mean that someone has been called homosexual by a friend or class mate, or that the individual is concerned about some supposedly "abnormal" physical characteristic. In most of my answers, I have tried to include reassurance as well as information. Sometimes a youngster may seem to be asking one thing when she or he is really asking something quite different. For example, "When is sex enjoyed the most?" may mean, "What situations make sex most enjoyable?" or "At what age does a person enjoy sex the most?" or "What is needed in a relationship for sex to be most enjoyable?" Sometimes a youngster of any age may ask questions to which you think he or she already knows the answers. The youngster is probably seeking reassurance, or may be testing you to see whether you are willing to discuss an embarrassing subject frankly and fully. In using this book, remember that young people need to be reminded constantly that they are normal, that their desires are healthy, that their behavior is common, that truly abnormal feelings or physical problems are rare.

Of course, this does not mean that you approve of that behavior, or that you think the young person should act on her or his desire. How you answer questions of what is right and what is wrong depends a great deal on your relationship with the young person in question. A teacher or school counsellor will probably be more hesitant to state absolutely what is proper and what is improper than a parent or a minister. However, even if you are absolutely sure what you think is morally correct in a given situation, it is usually better to postpone setting out absolute principles until you have listened sympathetically to the young person's viewpoint. As experienced adults, it is easy to think that we should be obeyed unquestioningly. Experience shows that young people, especially teenagers, often feel quite differently about this! Often it is best to respond to a question such as, "Is it OK for an unmarried teenager to have intercourse?" with a question like, "Well, what do you think?" Instead of "laying down the law," show the other person that you respect and are eager to hear his or her opinion; you may be surprised to find that it agrees with yours. Even if it doesn't, a teenager anxious to assert her or his independence will be far more likely to take your opinion seriously if you accord her or him the same respect. Remember that a young person may take a strong stand against you one day, only to completely change his or her mind the next.

The answers given are only suggestions; *they are not meant to be taken as the only right answers.* When you read them, you may find yourself thinking, "I would never answer that question that way." That's just fine—it means that you have already begun to work out your own answers. You need to be comfortable with the explanations you give children in your care. Moreover, if you give an answer that you are obviously uncomfortable with, the child will sense that you don't really believe what you are saying. You are probably better off avoiding a subject which you cannot discuss comfortably. But remember, it is usually wishful thinking to believe that, if you don't discuss a sexual practice which you find objectionable, the young person will not find out about it. Most of the time, if you don't respond to a child's question with enough accurate information, he or she will almost certainly try to learn more from friends—friends who are often badly misinformed. Too much information is probably better than too little, provided that you make it clear what your own feelings are about the sexual practices you are describing.

The book is divided into six chapters covering six topics related to sexuality and growing up. Within each topic, the questions are given roughly in order of progressing complexity and sophistication—it is not necessary (and probably not appropriate) to explain to an eight-year-old what an orgasm is or what forms sexual contact may take, when the general facts about how babies begin, where they develop and how they are born is all the information the child is seeking. Teenagers are more interested in the problems which sexually colored relationships raise, while these problems are usually of scant interest to younger children. Of course each reader of this book will have to adjust his or her answers to the sophistication and level of curiosity of the particular individual he or she is addressing. However, here are some general guidelines.

Children in pre-school and lower elementary school usually live very much in the present. Their curiosity about sexual behavior is not easily aroused, even when there are pet animals around who may engage in sex. Of course, they are curious about body parts and the differences between female and male anatomy, and frequently seek assurance that their bodies are normal. When questions concerning sexual intercourse or "where babies come from" arise, with young children I usually stress the role of intercourse in creating new people, not the pleasurable aspects. Many children, when they learn what sexual intercourse is, will ask "Why would anyone ever want to do that?" (I explain that it is necessary to make babies.)

Often a simple, one-sentence answer will satisfy a young child's curiosity.

It is important, however, to make it clear that you welcome the child's questions and will do your best to answer them. Young children can easily sense when their sexual questions are not welcomed, and can quickly learn that it is unacceptable to ask about the subjects of sex and their own bodies. If an answer is too complicated for them, they will take what they can get out of your answer. Later, they often come back with further questions to clear up what they found confusing—provided you have made it clear that further questions are always welcome. By reading stories to your children that have instances of teasing, hurt feelings, fighting you can stimulate many kinds of questions. Your local public or school librarian can be very helpful here.

Children in the upper elementary school grades increasingly ask questions about their development and about pregnancy and child birth. Their interest in sexual relationships and activity also increases. Many children at this age level are already curious about sexual intercourse and about homosexuality. Of less interest are birth control and sexually transmitted diseases (venereal diseases), with the exception of AIDS, which is frequently in the news. The child is usually seeking reassurance rather than detailed information. For some reason, fifth- and sixth-graders have a seemingly endless fascination with birth defects.

Children of middle-school (junior high school age) continue to be interested in physical development, pregnancy and child birth. Heredity is also of interest, as are sexual relationships and activity. Intercourse is a very frequent subject of lively interest. But at this age, there is much variation from child to child. Some seem merely to be curious, while for others the questions have more immediate significance as they become aware of their own sexuality. As they advance through these years, and their physical maturity is completed, their interest generally shifts from concern about bodily changes to concern about their sexual feelings and about relationships. They may begin to have close relationships with members of the opposite sex. Many of their questions show that they are beginning to regard sex as part of a relationship with another person, rather than just an activity you "do" like ice-skating.

Sexual practices also become an increasing area of concern toward the end of the middle school years. Here it is especially important to be willing to listen to the youngster's point of view. You must be willing to accept that young people—even your own children—may have different values from yours. But a general guiding principle I often put forth is,

Anything is all right in the area of sex as long as it does not hurt you or hurt the other person, and as long as it does not offend you or the other person.

This definition stresses responsibility to oneself, to one's sexual partner and to persons with different values.

It is especially important at this age to be aware of youngsters' needs for reassurance and to continue to let them know that you welcome their questions, and will try to answer them as honestly and fully as you can. For girls, menstruation is often a source of anxious concern, although this concern usually subsides once menstruation has actually commenced. Many young people, believe it or not, are already considering whether to have intercourse at this time, usually under pressure from friends. Some youngsters are already "street-wise" about sex, and have begun to experiment sexually. These children are especially prone to absorbing a great deal of misinformation about sex. So it is best to bring the risks involved to their attention. As they get older, their interest in birth control and sexually transmitted diseases increases. Youngsters of this age and on through their later teen years often want to hear that there is a form of contraception that is absolutely safe. When you tell them that only abstinence is 100% safe, they may think you are withholding information from them. It is important to keep reiterating this point. Similarly, they do not want to hear that teen sex during menstruation is **not** safe, or that interrupting intercourse or only placing the penis near the vagina are not reliable ways to prevent pregnancy. Although questions about sexual diseases may not be very frequent for children just entering middle school, it is a good idea to bring them to young people's attention. Here, as in drug problems, scare tactics are not usually effective. It is better to give the facts as simply as possible, and then invite the young person to explain how he or she would avoid the risks involved.

Children of this age are also very interested in heredity. This provides a good opportunity for you to bring up the drug problem by discussing the effects of illegal drugs on babies growing in the womb. At this age and for long after, young people often have the feeling that "nothing bad is ever going to happen to me," and this is as good a time as any to begin to challenge that assumption—not only with respect to drugs, but with respect to pregnancy and sexually transmitted diseases as well.

Many high school students are fully developed physically or will finish their growth before graduation. Many of these individuals have lost interest in the academic side of school (witness the high dropout rate). There is great importance placed on "going steady." Unfortunately this locks the young person into a relationship and keeps him or her from experiencing relationships that would be helpful in his or her development.

Having a peer group to belong to is also important to the teenager. Often it seems that the only time the student is truly alive is when he or she has a chance to meet his or her friends between and after classes.

Parents say their older teenagers ask very few questions about sex, and that it is difficult to start a conversation with them. The teenagers often seem defensive about many things. Taking a situation from television or the movies and asking the teenagers for their opinions may help begin a discussion. Listening to their opinions and thanking them afterward for sharing their opinions with you may be a novel experience and make it easier for them to open up next time.

Sometimes trust must be established all over again on a more mature level. You could offer to go to the Planned Parenthood clinic with your teenager(s) to learn about contraceptives. Your teenager will probably not wish you to accompany him or her but just the fact that you offered will demonstrate your confidence in him or her to make a good decision. One parent told me that she discussed contraceptives with her daughter (in fear and trembling) and when she had finished, her daughter said, "Well, now I know so nobody can talk me into doing something I don't want to do."

High school students also hold the belief that "nothing bad is ever going to happen to me." Teenagers' self-esteem still needs a good deal of bolstering. They feel grown up but are not allowed to be adults. As a parent, try to find five things every day that you can compliment your teenager about. Tell your daughter or son over and over what you like about his or her looks and what he or she is doing. You may think the teenager will feel you are overdoing it, but he or she never does. Studies show that people with high self-esteem make better decisions for themselves. We all function better in life when we feel good about ourselves.

Questions from older teenagers are usually about relationships. There are many questions about respect, manipulation, power struggle and using or being used by another person. All of these complicated situations are very puzzling to a teenager. Sol Gordon has a book about "lines" that can be very helpful as well as entertaining. Soap operas are full of situations that are destructive in relationships—some teenagers actually believe this is the way a person is supposed to act in a relationship.

FRANCES YOUNGER

CONTENTS

FIVE HUNDRED QUESTIONS KIDS ASK ABOUT SEX

And Some of the Answers

Chapter I

BODILY DEVELOPMENT
AND SEXUAL MATURATION

A. GENERAL BODILY DEVELOPMENT

1 How tall will I be when I grow up?

There is no way to know for sure ahead of time. You will probably be a little taller or shorter than your parents—perhaps an inch or two. The genetic pattern you inherited from your parents will determine this.

2 Why do some people grow faster than others?

Each person has his or her own timetable for growing up. For the first two to three years, children grow very rapidly. Then they settle down to an inch or an inch and one-half per year until their pre-teens. At that time they start to grow in spurts—a rapid growth of several inches in a few months, followed by months or even a whole year in which there is very little change in height. Then they have another spurt. If you are between spurts, don't worry; your growth will start up again before long!

3 When will I reach my full adult height?

Girls usually finish growing by the time they are sixteen years old. Boys take a little longer—until they are twenty to twenty-two years old.

4 How do we grow?

We grow by cell division. The body is made up of billions of tiny cells. Each cell has some specific function: muscle cells to contract, blood cells to carry oxygen and fight infection, tongue cells to taste, brain cells to think and so forth. But most cells in the body also reproduce, that is, make another cell just like themselves. They do this both to enable the body to grow and to replace cells that die.

To grow, these cells need the nutrients necessary to produce more of themselves. During our growing years, it is especially important for us to eat well balanced diets.

5 Why does my daddy have so much hair on his chest?

Many men have a great deal of hair on their chests. Some have only a little, and some have almost none. Just as some people have long noses, some short ones, so some men have a lot of hair, some have only a little. Each of us is unique—when you grow up you will resemble your parents

7

in some ways, but in others you will not. Body hair is one of the inherited traits you receive from your parents.

6 How do animals go to the bathroom?

Every kind of animal has some means of getting rid of its waste products. They all have a small opening for eliminating urine, and another for defecation (eliminating solid waste). Sometimes you can train an animal to urinate and defecate in a special place such as a litter box for a cat, or to wait to go until it is outside, as with a dog. With some animals, such as birds, you cannot.

7 Do the intestines grow as the body grows?

The intestines are made up of a long tube that is folded up inside the body and connected to the stomach at one end and to the anus at the other. The intestines take the partially digested food from the stomach and help the body to absorb the nutrients so that the body can receive nourishment. All of the parts of the body grow together. Like the outside which we can see, the inside changes and grows larger.

8 What is the rectum? What is a bowel movement?

The rectum is the opening at the end of the large intestine. This opening is located between the two large folds of muscle and skin called the buttocks or behind. It allows for bowel movements, or solid waste material, to be discharged from the body. This material consists mostly of what is left over after the body has removed the nutrients it needs from the food you eat, during digestion. Digestion takes place in the stomach and small intestine.

It is important to discharge waste from the body. Most people have a regular cycle for eliminating solid waste—every day or every two days, depending on an individual's cycle. If you have difficulty with your bowel movements, drink more water, and eat high fiber foods like fruits and vegetables, bran and oat cereals and dark grain breads.

9 Why does your face and hair get oily during the teen years?

You will notice that your body is secreting oil both on your face and on your scalp. This results from the rapid growth and changes your body is undergoing. It is important to wash your face well to avoid getting pimples or at least to keep them under control. You can also wash your hair daily if you find that the oiliness makes you too uncomfortable. There are special shampoos for oily hair that you might try.

10 What can drugs do to your body?

Any chemical taken into the body is a drug. But we are talking about such illegal substances as "crack," cocaine, heroin, "speed," "uppers" and "downers," LSD and marijuana. These drugs can all be very harmful to the body. "Crack," cocaine, heroin, speed, uppers and downers can all kill. "Crack" is now an especially bad problem, because it is highly addictive and even one use can cause sudden death. Most of these drugs may also interfere with your sexual ability.

If someone you know tells you what great fun it is and that it won't hurt you, don't believe it! This person needs help. If you are tempted to use these or other illegal drugs, talk it over instead with your parents, a trusted teacher, your school counsellor, your minister or rabbi. They will not share the information with anyone if you ask them not to.

11 What is "mono"?

"Mono" is short for infectious mononucleosis. It is a disease caused by a virus. It can be spread from one person to another, even from someone who does not have the disease symptoms but is a carrier. Sometimes it is called the "kissing disease," because it can be spread by kissing.

"Mono" can be relatively mild, or it can make you very sick, even threatening your life. The most common symptom is feeling tired all the time, even when you have had a lot of sleep. If the tired feeling continues for several weeks or if you are tired for no apparent reason, you need to check with your doctor.

This disease, like most viral diseases, cannot be cured by any drug treatment. You just have to get plenty of rest and wait until your body's immune system builds up resistance to it and drives the infection out of your body. The best defense against catching mononucleosis is to keep your body healthy by eating good foods, getting proper exercise and sleeping enough.

B. SEXUAL CHARACTERISTICS
AND THEIR DEVELOPMENT

12 Why do boys look different from girls?

Each body has special chemicals called hormones directing it to develop into a male or female body. It has inherited chromosomes or genes from its parents that will direct how it will develop.

When a baby is first born, the parents can tell whether it is a boy or girl by seeing whether it has a penis and testicles, or a vagina. Even though this is the only obvious difference between girl babies and boy babies, they will grow up to look different in a number of ways. Boys are generally taller and more muscular while girls have prominent breasts and more rounded hips. Men have thick hair on their faces, arms and legs and sometimes on the chest, while women do not. Men usually have deep voices, women higher ones. Women have an extra layer of body fat under their skins that men lack.

13 Do girls' bodies have anything in common with boys' bodies?

Yes, they certainly do. In fact, they are more alike than different. They both have the same kind of brain, the same number of bones, the same kind of blood, skin, heart, lungs, etc. The only major differences are in their sexual organs, in musculature and in body shape.

Often it seems that girls and boys differ in their talents and abilities. But they were not born that way; rather it is because they were brought up to think that it's not "feminine" or "masculine" to do certain things. For example, it's obvious that boys can learn to sew and that girls can pilot aircraft, for many men and women do both these activities. Until recently, it was thought that boys who sewed or girls who piloted aircraft had something wrong with them. Fortunately this view has been disappearing in recent years.

14 Why do boys have penises and girls vaginas?

These organs are essential to having children. The penis enables a man to become a father. The vagina enables a woman to become a mother. From adolescence on the boy's testicles produce sperm that can start a baby growing in a woman. During sexual intercourse, the man places his firm penis into the woman's vagina, and millions of sperm leave the penis and enter the woman's vagina. If the sperm meet an egg, a baby is started. Nine months later the baby comes back out of the vagina. The penis is also used for urination. The girl urinates from a small opening close to the vagina.

15 What do the sexual parts of boys and girls look like?

Most likely you have seen the sexual organs of baby boys and girls. The boy has a penis and testicles between his legs. The penis is small and shaped like the end of your finger. The boy urinates through an opening in the tip of his penis. Behind the penis there is a sack of skin called the scrotum, which holds two almond-shaped or oval organs called the testicles.

The girl has a vagina between her legs. It has two folds of skin, called the **labia** or lips. These cover two small openings, one smaller than the other. The smaller opening is for urine to come out. The other opening is the entrance to a tube called the vagina that goes up to the uterus.

16 How do boys and girls urinate (pee)? Why do boys do it standing up, while girls sit down?

"Pee" is a slang term for urination. A boy usually urinates standing in front of the toilet. He directs his penis so that the urine streams out of it into the toilet. A girl usually sits down on the toilet seat to keep from getting urine on the rest of her body. A boy can "aim" his urine flow but a girl cannot.

17 Why do older boys and girls have hair around their sex organs?

We really don't know. We know why we have hair on our heads—to keep us warm in cold weather. But we really don't know why hair grows on other parts of the body. Both boys and girls grow **pubic** hair around their private parts—in front and between their legs.

Anthropologists tell us that thousands of years ago, the ancestors of human beings were almost completely covered with hair. This was probably protection from the cold. As human beings emerged, they began to wear clothing, and so had less need for body hair. Through the process of evolution, body hair decreased. The entire body is covered with fine hair—some people have more or less than others. It grows heavier on certain parts of the body. It grows on the head, the arms and underarms, the legs, on the face for men and for both men and women around the sex organs between the legs.

18 Will I develop just like my friends?

No. Each girl and boy has his or her own timetable for growing up. Even in the same family, no two children grow up in just the same way. Some boys and girls begin to grow up and change when they are ten or twelve years old. Others do not start until they are fifteen or sixteen years old. This is all within a normal range. But by the time they are about twenty years old, all boys and girls grow up into young men and women. You may feel worried or upset if some of your friends grow up before you do. That is their timetable, controlled by their genes. Your genes will control your unique timetable, one that is just right for you.

19 At what age do boys and girls begin puberty?

Puberty is the time during which boys and girls develop into men and women. Girls start changing into women at about age nine or ten, and are finished between sixteen and eighteen years of age. Boys may start to change as young as ten, but most boys don't begin changing until they are twelve to fourteen years old. They finish between ages twenty and twenty-two. So at high school graduation, most girls have probably finished developing, while many boys may still be in transition.

This difference in development timing means that for about two or three years, most girls are taller than most boys. But this is only a temporary situation; soon the boys catch up and grow taller than the girls.[1]

20 When they reach their teens, why do girls start to look more like their mothers, and boys start to look more like their fathers?

Built into a newborn baby's body are special instructions, called genes. Perhaps you are surprised to learn that babies are born with genes on, since you thought they were born naked! But these genes are not pants that you wear; they are very tiny parts of every cell in your body—far too tiny to see. The genes hold the instructions that tell the body how to develop in every way: what color eyes and hair it will have, how tall it will be, whether it will have a big nose or floppy ears—in fact, without the instructions from the genes, the body would not even grow eyes or a nose or ears at all!

You grew from the genes you received from your father and mother. That is why you probably look quite a bit like both of them. But you will never look exactly like either one of your parents, because you have some genes from your mother, some from your father, and **they** do not look like each other.

The genes also tell the body what sex it is. While the baby is still inside the mother, they tell the baby's body to grow a vagina or penis, and the other sex organs as well as every other part of the body. But their work is not done once the baby is born. The genes continue to tell the body how to grow throughout life, and also control the timing of these developments. They send their instructions to the body through chemicals that are circulated in the bloodstream. Somewhere between the boy's tenth and fourteenth birthdays, the genes tell his body to develop larger muscles and heavier hair on the face, arms and legs. At about the age nine or ten years, the girl's genes tell her breasts to grow larger, to develop rounded hips, to grow extra body fat and to begin menstruating. The period of these changes is called puberty. All of these changes take eight to ten years and are completed by the time a woman is sixteen to eighteen years old, a boy twenty to twenty-two years of age. For more on heredity and the genes, see the section on Heredity.

21 Why do girls mature sooner than boys?

We don't know for sure why this difference in timing exists, but it probably helped early human beings survive under hostile conditions. Many children died, and those who survived childhood only lived to about age forty as recently as one hundred years ago. Early maturation of women enabled them to produce many babies, thereby guaranteeing that some would grow to reach adulthood, and the mother could live long enough to raise them. Boys, on the other hand, may have entered puberty slightly later to give them time both to grow stronger and to learn to hunt and fight, so that they could protect their families. In tribal societies, where survival is still uncertain, the boy is taken into the tribe when he is about twelve years old, and taught the skills he needs to keep himself and his family alive. Only after he learns them is he allowed to take a wife.

In our society, of course, the situation is rather different. We can expect the overwhelming majority of children to survive to adulthood, so early and frequent childbearing is no longer necessary. But we cannot change our biological clocks, which took their present form hundreds of thousands of years ago.

The ultimate controllers of all development are the genes, which tell the body how and when to grow in every aspect. Sexual development however is stimulated by the pituitary gland, located in the brain. Following genetic instructions, it controls the release of special chemicals called **hormones** into the blood. These chemicals tell the girl's body to begin maturing at about ten to twelve years of age and the boy at twelve to fourteen years of age.

C. FORMS OF SEXUAL ACTIVITY

22 What is sexual intercourse? How do you have sexual intercourse? Is there a right way and a wrong way?

In sexual intercourse, a man inserts his erect penis into the woman's vagina. During intercourse, the contact of penis and vagina usually produces intensely pleasurable sexual pleasure for both the man and woman. This intense stimulation can lead either or both of them to have an orgasm. (See the question 26 ON ORGASM, below.) When the man has an orgasm he ejaculates millions of sperm into the vagina. When a woman has an orgasm, the opening to her uterus, the cervix, dips into the pool of sperm that the man has deposited. However, a woman who has not had an orgasm during intercourse can also easily become pregnant. The sperm then travel through the uterus and into the fallopian tubes. If even one sperm reaches a ripe egg as the egg is traveling down one of the tubes, it becomes fertilized and a new life begins. However, there are many ways to have intercourse while preventing fertilization or conception from taking place. These are discussed in the chapter on contraception.

There are no "right" or "wrong" ways to have intercourse—some ways are more comfortable and satisfying than others. Over the centuries many books have been written about this subject. Some are available in book stores and libraries where you can read them.

23 Does sexual intercourse hurt?

Normally it does not. However, it could hurt for several reasons. The first time, it may hurt because the woman's maidenhead or hymen may be broken when the man's penis is inserted. When this happens, a small amount of bleeding is likely to occur. Usually the hymen has been stretched or broken long before the first time the woman has sex. The hyman is a piece of skin stretched over most of the opening to the vagina.

Intercourse may also be painful because the woman is not fully sexually aroused and her vagina is not moist enough. This may be because she or her partner are in too much of a hurry to have intercourse. The woman may also not be fully aroused because she is anxious or feels guilty about having intercourse. She may, for example, fear that she will become pregnant. In this situation, the muscles of her vagina may tighten up, making insertion of the penis difficult and painful.

24 How far can the man's penis go into the woman's vagina?

The vagina is usually from three to five inches long in a fully grown woman. It is very flexible and can stretch and become somewhat longer. A teenage girl's vagina may not have reached mature size, making intercourse more painful. A man cannot injure a woman because he puts his penis in "too far." A strong muscular wall is at the end of the vagina that prevents this.

25 What happens if the penis becomes stuck inside the vagina?

This is an extremely rare occurrence in human beings, although you may have seen it happen in dogs. If a woman's vaginal muscles were to become painfully tight, the man would soon lose his erection and easily withdraw his penis.

Of course, if a woman is tense for any reason, these muscles can tighten and make intercourse very painful for her. If this happens, the man should not attempt to enter her or continue to have intercourse, as he may hurt the woman.

26 What is an orgasm? Is it true that girls "come" when having sex?

Sexual activity produces a build up of sexual feelings. If it is continued long enough, these feelings reach a peak and are then released, producing an experience of intense sexual pleasure and release. This sensation of pleasure and release is called an orgasm. A slang term for orgasm is "coming." It is a very special feeling, and no one experiences it in quite the same way.

An orgasm is centered in the sexual organs; in the penis in a man, and in the clitoris in a woman, and also is felt strongly in the muscles of the vagina and uterus. But it affects the entire body. Both men and women can have orgasms during sexual activity, including sexual intercourse.

In a man, ejaculation usually occurs at the same time as an orgasm. In a woman, an orgasm produces movements in the uterus that make fertilization more likely. (But it is very easy for a woman who has not had an orgasm during intercourse to get pregnant.)

Women often have more difficulty in reaching orgasm than men. This can be due to a variety of factors. The most important is society's continuing double standard, in which male sexual pleasure is thought to be normal, while female sexual pleasure is still thought to be somehow "wrong" or "unfeminine." This attitude has changed greatly in the last few years, but old attitudes take a long time to disappear.

If there is difficulty, often one partner can help the other to reach orgasm by stroking his or her partner's sexual organs with the fingers. Another important factor affecting both female and male sexual pleasure is the conditions in which sexual activity takes place. The lack of a feeling of affection and trust between you and your partner may make it difficult to relax and enjoy this most intimate of experiences. The fear that you may be interrupted at any moment, the fear of pregnancy, a lack of confidence in your birth control method (or a lack of any method) can also make it very difficult for both you and your partner to really enjoy sex.

27 What is masturbation? Do women as well as men masturbate? Is it all right to masturbate?

Masturbation involves stroking one's own sexual organs, often until one experiences an orgasm. In the man it involves stroking the penis, while in the woman it involves stroking the lips of the vagina and the clitoris. Doctors tell us that masturbation does no harm to the sexual organs.

It is acceptable to masturbate in private, so long as you feel comfortable doing it. However, masturbation in public is considered embarrassing to other people. It can even lead to criminal charges, so it is important to do it only in private. It is also important not to allow masturbation to become a substitute for social activities with friends of both sexes, or interfere with your school work.

It is a myth that boys or men can use up all their sperm through masturbation or frequent intercourse. See the question 47 on can a man run out of sperm.

28 What does it mean to say "he ate her out?"

"Eating her out" is a slang term for oral sexual activity in which a man stimulates a woman's vagina and clitoris by contact with his mouth and tongue. A woman can also engage in oral sexual activity by stimulating a man's penis with her mouth and tongue. The slang term for this is a "blow job."

These activities can be pleasurable under the right circumstances, but you should not allow yourself to be pressured into doing something you are not comfortable with—as with any form of sexual activity.

A woman cannot get pregnant from these activities, but both men and women can contract sexually transmitted diseases from them. The penis, the vagina, the throat and the rectum are the bodily openings where sexually transmitted disease germs can enter, live and in turn be transmitted to someone else.

29 If a woman gives several men a blow job, can she get some kind of disease?

A woman can catch a sexually transmitted disease by orally stimulating a man's penis, and the more men she does it with, the more likely she is to encounter one with a disease.

30 What do you think about anal sex? Can a man have intercourse with a woman in her butt?

Anal sex involves a man placing his penis in his partner's rectum, through the anus. (The anus is the opening from which solid waste material is expelled.) It is common among homosexual men, but may be frequently practiced between men and women. Like other activities, it can be pleasurable if both partners are willing, but no one should feel obligated to do it.

Anal intercourse is something that must be done carefully, because the anus, and the part of the intestine just inside it (called the rectum) is not flexible like the vagina and has many blood vessels within its tissue. The person could easily be hurt if force or lack of lubrication is used. It is also a way of contracting a sexually transmitted disease.

31 Can a woman get pregnant from anal penetration?

No. The sperm cannot go from the anus and rectum to the uterus, to cause a pregnancy. While anal sex cannot lead to pregnancy, it can transmit sexually transmitted diseases.

32 What is spanish fly?

Spanish fly is a powder made from a dead beetle that is supposed to be an aphrodisiac. An aphrodisiac is anything that increases sexual desire or arousal. Spanish fly was very popular years ago. It was supposed to bring about an erection after being applied to the penis as an ointment. It seemed to irritate the area, and may have caused lasting harm.

Most things sold to increase sexual desire or ability are frauds. They are aphrodisiacs only for the people who make and sell them. With the money they have made by deceiving others, they can impress their girl friends or boy friends with fancy dinners and expensive wines that put them in the mood for sex!

Spanish fly is very toxic **and should never be used as a drink.**

D. MALE SEXUAL DEVELOPMENT AND FUNCTION

33 Why does my penis get hard sometimes? What is a "hard-on?" What is a "boner?"

Although most of the time the penis is small and just hangs there, the penis has the special ability to become longer and very hard. This change is called an erection. Slang terms for this are "hard-on" or "boner." "Boner" probably refers to the fact that the penis appears to have a bone inside it during an erection. In reality there is no bone. Some of the tissue which makes up the penis is spongelike. In an erection the spaces become filled with blood, causing the penis to become stiff and erect.

Usually, an erection is in response to some kind of sexual stimulation. Your brain sorts out all sorts of stimuli, both from your own imagination and from your eyes, ears, nose and skin. When you see or smell tasty food, it sends messages to your stomach to make you feel hungry. When you hear a sudden noise, it sends messages to your muscles that make you jump. When you see or think about sexual things, it sends messages to your body that make you feel sexual desire and that tell your penis to have an erection.

Sometimes a boy may see a girl or woman, and will think sexy thoughts about her. Sometimes he may simply think such thoughts about a girl who isn't even there. Sometimes a picture on television, in the movies or in a magazine may trigger sexy thoughts. All of these things can cause an erection. So too can contact with a girl or woman — anything from brushing against a stranger on a bus, to holding a friend's hand, to kissing or other kinds of intimate contact. Touching the man's penis will also often lead to an erection. If a boy or man handles his own penis, he will probably have an erection.

An erection prepares the penis for sexual intercourse, to enter a woman's vagina and deposit sperm there. An erection usually also increases the desire to have intercourse. But this does not mean that every time a boy or man has an erection he must have intercourse! Contrary to what some people may say, there is no unbearable suffering for a boy or man who has an erection but does not have intercourse! A few minutes after sexual stimulation has stopped, the erection will fade away.

A man can also have an erection for other reasons. The penis often responds to both internal and external conditions by becoming firm. In the morning, when a boy needs to urinate, it may become firm. If the boy gets into the shower or bathtub it may get firm. If a boy becomes tense or excited, it may become erect. Sometimes it seems to have a mind of its own. This is nothing to worry about; that is just the way it acts!

34 What is a normal sized penis? Is my penis too small? When will my penis start to grow bigger?

Every man's penis is just a little bit different from every other. This is not surprising, seeing that no two people's eyes, nose, ears, hands, or feet are exactly alike or exactly the same size. Just as some boys are taller than others, or have bigger noses, some boys' penises are bigger than others. Some penises are as much as seven inches long, while others are smaller. Some penises grow much more than others at puberty. This is determined by heredity.

Many people think that a man with a bigger penis can have better intercourse or give more pleasure to the woman. Boys with smaller penises may often be kidded by other boys who believe the old myth that a large penis makes one "more of a man."

These ideas are simply false. The fact is that a man with a very small penis is just as capable of a good, firm erection and of giving sexual pleasure to a woman as one with a large penis. During an erection a small penis will stretch more to reach its full length, while a large penis will simply not stretch much when it becomes firm. There is not much difference in size once they have become erect. When a penis is firm and erect, it is five to seven inches long. If you have seen pictures in magazines of men with twelve-inch penises, this is just trick photography. Since women's vaginas are at most about five inches long, every man's penis can fill every woman's vagina. They fit together very well!

If you are having regular intercourse and you or your partner are not experiencing much pleasure, the problem almost certainly has to do with your feelings about each other and about sex, not with your sex organs. For more information, refer to the relationships chapter.[2]

35 What is impotence?

Impotence means that the man is unable to have a lasting erection, and so cannot have satisfactory and enjoyable intercourse with a woman. It is often the result of emotional tensions that the man needs to talk over with his partner, a trusted friend, a doctor, professional counsellor or minister. It may also be a symptom of some health problem or a reaction to a certain medication. If it happens again and again, a doctor should be consulted.

Impotence is very rare in teenagers.

36 Why are some male babies circumcised?

Circumcision involves cutting off a piece of the skin on the end of the penis called the foreskin. Since it is an operation, it may hurt the baby for a brief time.

It originated as a religious practice among Jews and other religious groups. In more recent times, it is performed because it is thought to prevent infections, but this is now questioned by many doctors.

You can tell you are circumcised if the tip of the penis is exposed, with the fold of skin somewhat back from the tip. You are not circumcised if the skin is tight around the tip or extends over the tip a small amount. Being circumcised and not being circumcised are both quite normal. All uncircumcised men need to be sure to wash under the foreskin.

37 What is the white stuff that comes out of my penis? What is an ejaculation?

This is the seminal fluid which contains the sperm. It comes out during an ejaculation. This happens when the male is strongly aroused sexually, usually at the same time as an orgasm (see Question 26). However, a small amount, containing many active sperm, often comes out before an orgasm. It is important for boys and girls and men and women to know this, because it is the reason that withdrawal or stopping intercourse just before ejaculation doesn't always prevent pregnancy.

During intercourse, the seminal fluid carries the sperm into the woman's vagina, so that the sperm can begin their journey upward to fertilize an ovum (egg). Often it comes out at night during a nocturnal emission, a "wet dream" or during masturbation. This is all normal.

38 What happens in an ejaculation?

First the penis becomes erect (see Erection in the Glossary). Then the sperm leave the testicles, mix with seminal fluid in the prostate gland and travel the length of the penis, leaving at the tip. The sperm and fluid are forced out by four or five contractions of muscles in and behind the penis. There can be a million or more sperm in one ejaculation.

Urine and sperm cannot come out at the same time. There is a cut-off valve that makes it difficult for urine to come out when the penis is erect.

39 What causes an ejaculation?

An ejaculation, like an erection, is usually caused by some kind of sexual stimulation. Prolonged physical stimulation, such as intercourse or masturbation, will usually produce an ejaculation. A nocturnal emission or "wet dream" is also an ejaculation (see Question 44 on wet dreams).

40 Is there a limit to how many times a man can ejaculate?

Yes, there seems to be a limit. After one ejaculation, the penis does not respond to any sexual stimulation for awhile. The man's body seems to need a short recovery period before another ejaculation can take place. Different men have different abilities to ejaculate at different times in their lives. Some can only do so or only wish to do so once during a single period of sexual activity, while others can do so several times. Often both sexual partners may think there is little to be done to improve the man's sexual ability, but there are techniques for increasing the number of times a man can ejaculate, just as there are techniques for enabling a woman who has difficulty experiencing orgasms to get more pleasure from sex.

When a man cannot ejaculate at all, this indicates some kind of problem. He may just be very tense. But drugs or some health problems can also interfere with his sexual ability. If this problem persists, a doctor should be consulted.

41 What is the scrotum and what are the testicles for? Where are sperm produced?

The scrotum is part of the male genitals or sex organs. It is a sack located between the legs, below and behind the penis. The scrotum holds the two round organs called the testicles.

The testicles are the organs that produce sperm. They can easily be felt as hard, marble-sized balls in the scrotum. Sometimes one is slightly larger than the other. Only one healthy testicle is needed to produce all the children a man could ever want to have.

The scrotum has a very interesting function. It regulates the temperature of the testicles. The testicles cannot produce sperm at the normal body temperature, so the scrotum keeps them a little cooler by holding them away from the body. On a warm day, it becomes a little longer, so that the testicles are further from the body. On a cold day, it becomes smaller to bring the testicles nearer the body. After a swim, a boy will notice that his scrotum has become very small, because the water is usually too cold for the testicles to function properly. But in a warm bath, this will not happen.

In some boys, the testicle may not always be present in the scrotum. If it is never present, it may be inside the body and is called an undescended testicle. This condition requires medical attention, because the testicle cannot develop properly inside the body, as the body's temperature is too high.

42 How big are sperm cells? Where are they produced?

They are very tiny and can only be seen with the aid of a microscope. Eight hundred thousand fit on the head of a pin, yet only one of them is needed to fertilize an egg and set in motion a new life. The egg is much larger—about the size of a pin head. The sperm are produced in the testicles, which are connected by tubes to the penis. It takes about six weeks for them to mature.

During ejaculation, about two hundred million sperm travel out of the testicles and into the body, where they pick up other substances that form the seminal fluid. This fluid protects the sperm and gives them energy. Then the fluid carries the sperm through the penis and out of the body.

The sperm contain genes, the even smaller units that will tell the new baby how to grow. Together with the genes from one of the mother's eggs, the genes in one sperm cell will tell the baby's body how to develop. (That is why a child resembles both its mother and father.) For more on the functioning of the genes, see the section on heredity.

43 When does a boy begin to produce sperm? At what age can a boy get a girl pregnant? How can a boy tell if he has begun to produce sperm?

The boy's body begins to produce sperm cells when he is about eleven or twelve years old. Once a boy has begun to produce sperm he can get a girl pregnant. How can he tell? He will notice that a white fluid comes out of his penis either during masturbation or during the night in a "wet dream" or nocturnal emission. Nocturnal emissions are a sure sign that a boy is producing sperm and seminal fluids.

44 What is a "wet dream"?

"Wet dream" is a slang term for a nocturnal emission. What happens is that the penis becomes firm, and the white fluid called semen—which contains millions of sperm—is forced from the tip (ejaculation). This happens at night when a boy is relaxed or sleeping. Most boys have nocturnal emissions from the time they are 11 or 12 years old. They may continue to have them for the rest of their lives. They may happen as often as once a week, depending upon how frequently the individual engages in other forms of sexual release, and how fast his body produces sperm.

This is an automatic process—you cannot make yourself have a nocturnal emission, and you cannot stop one from happening. They are not the result of "bad" thoughts or too much thinking about sex. The body is constantly producing new sperm, and does this to expel excess sperm and fluid. The boy may wake up during the nocturnal emission or sleep right through it. It doesn't hurt, and in fact can feel quite pleasurable. It may or may not be combined with a dream.

45 Do girls have wet dreams?

No, girls do not have nocturnal emissions. The girl's body does not constantly produce eggs or ova; it usually releases one per month, which her body discharges during menstruation if she does not become pregnant. But girls and women can have sexy dreams, just as boys and men do.

46 How long do sperm live outside the body? Is it true that they die when they reach the air?

Sperm can live for several hours outside the man's body if they are surrounded with semen and kept at body temperature. But they cannot live in bathtub water, on the skin or on a sheet because there they are separated from the moist semen that protects them and supplies them with nourishment.

However, it is possible for sperm to live right outside the vagina where it is warm and moist—they may certainly live long enough to find their way into the vagina, and from there travel upward until they encounter an egg to fertilize. This is how a girl can be a "pregnant virgin;" she has never had intercourse, but she has become pregnant because a man placed his penis near her vagina, although not in it. Any time a man places his erect penis near a woman's vagina, there is a chance that she could become pregnant.

47 How much sperm can a man produce?

There are several million sperm in every ejaculation. Only a tiny, tiny fraction of these sperm ever encounter an egg, usually most sperm are ejaculated when a fertile egg is unavailable or contraception prevents fertilization. The overwhelming majority of sperm die without ever fertilizing an egg. Nature produces vastly more sperm than could ever be used. But this very excess assures that more than enough eggs do get fertilized to guarantee that our species continues to survive and prosper.

48 Can a man ever run out of sperm? Can a 65-year-old man still father children?

A man never runs out of sperm, unless he has a disease that interferes with sperm production. Even elderly men may father children. After several expulsions of sperm (ejaculations) close together the man's sperm count—the number of sperm in a drop of semen—may temporarily become lower. But it will soon go back up to its normal number.

This is why masturbation is not physically harmful. Frequent masturbation may temporarily reduce the sperm count, but very soon more will be produced. You have no need to fear that your sperm supply will be used up before you are ready to become a father.

49 Will I ever lose my penis?

No, you will not. It is part of your body and will not come off! It can hurt a lot if you bump yourself in that area, especially in the testicles, but in most cases the pain will go away in a little while and there is usually no permanent harm.

50 Can a man's testicles crack if he is kicked very hard?

No, they cannot. But any blow to the testicles is extremely painful. A serious injury or repeated blows to the testicles may cause them to function improperly or not at all. A boy who is struck in the groin area and continues to feel pain after a few days should consult a doctor.

51 Why does my chest get sore and swell? It looks like I am growing breasts.

This development is called breast knots. It is a part of your development. The glands in your chest are developing. No, you are not developing breasts. This tenderness will go away in a short time.

E. FEMALE SEXUAL DEVELOPMENT AND FUNCTION

52 Why do girls have breasts?

Breasts are the two glands that are located on the chest and are marked by the nipples. Boys and girls, men and women have breasts, but in women they are usually much larger. In girls, they first begin to grow larger during the early teens, at puberty. They are usually fully developed by about sixteen years of age.

The breasts' function in women is to provide milk to feed the baby. The baby sucks on the mother's nipples to get the milk that the breasts produce and store. A newborn baby can only drink mother's milk or specially prepared formulas. It cannot eat the food that the rest of us eat. Mother's milk is especially good for the baby since it contains special substances called antibodies that help the baby avoid getting sick. Breast milk is easier for the baby to digest, thus lessening the baby's chances of getting an upset stomach or gas pains. Formulas and store-bought milk do not contain these antibodies.

Human beings, along with monkeys, dogs, cats, cows, horses and many other animals, are said to be **mammals.** The breasts are also called the **mammary** glands. All mammals have breasts and nurse their young. Birds, fish, snakes and frogs are not classified as mammals because they do not nurse their young.

53 When do girls' breasts or "tits" begin to grow large?

"Tits" is a slang term for breasts. It is insulting to girls and women. Teats applies to the nipples of a cow.

The breasts of some girls begin to develop as early as nine years of age, while in others, they don't begin until sixteen years of age. These ages, and everything in between, are completely normal. The timing of development, as well as the size and shape of the breasts, are set by the growing pattern a girl inherits and is set in her genes.

In some cases a hormone deficiency may cause a problem. If you are nearing the age of sixteen years or so and have yet to begin to develop, you probably should consult a physician.

54 How big can a girl's breasts become?

Breasts come in many different shapes and sizes. Like everything else, your breast size is determined by heredity. To some extent, being overweight increases the breast size, but this is a very unhealthy way to make your breasts bigger, because being overweight may contribute to some health problems, such as high blood pressure or heart disease.

No matter what size your breasts are, they will be more than adequate for feeding your babies. They will become larger when you are pregnant, then return to their regular size after you stop nursing. Both small and large breasts are equally capable of experiencing the pleasure of sexual caressing, and many boys and men will find you attractive whatever your breast size is. One man may find large breasts especially attractive, while another may be "turned on" by a more petite figure.

55 How do girls' breasts grow?

Girls have chemicals called hormones in their bloodstream stimulated by the pituitary gland that tell their breast cells to divide. Boys may experience a short period of swelling, sometimes accompanied by soreness, in their chests due to normal hormonal changes as they mature. These are called breast-knots, and are only temporary. The boy does not have to worry that he is developing womanly breasts.

56 Why don't I have a "dickie"?

"Dickie" is a slang term for penis. Only boys have penises, while girls have vaginas. See question 14 on the purposes of vaginas in girls and penises in boys.

57 Why can't boys have babies?

Boys and men cannot have babies because they do not have the necessary organs: ovaries, the uterus and the vagina. Fathers may share the experience of being a parent by assisting and supporting their wives through the experience of pregnancy, giving birth, nursing and sharing in the joys of watching their children grow up.

58 Why don't boys develop large breasts?

Boys' breasts do not grow large because boys are not going to become mothers and nurse babies. A boy's genes do not cause messages to be sent to his breasts that would make them develop, because he does not need them.

59 How big does the vagina get? How much can it stretch?

Its length is usually three to five inches. Its width is about three-fourths of an inch, but it has a truly amazing ability to expand. It is very flexible. During sexual intercourse it easily widens to hold a man's erect penis. During childbirth it widens much more, to allow the baby's head to pass through (the head and shoulders are the widest parts of a baby's body). After the baby is born, it returns to its normal size.[3]

60 What is a douche? Should women douche?

A douche is a bath of the vagina. The woman uses a small tube to squirt the fluid into the vaginal tube.

Douching is usually unnecessary, since the vagina has fluid inside it that keeps it clean and free of infection and odor most of the time. Many companies promote douching through advertising on television and in magazines. Often they play on a woman's fears of having an unpleasant bodily odor. But normal washing of the genital area with soap and water will prevent this. Douching makes money for the companies, but does little for a woman who has no health problem with her sexual organs.

It is only necessary to douche if a doctor tells you to, usually because of some medical problem. The doctor or nurse practitioner will instruct you as to what type of douche to use.

61 What is a "cherry?" What does "pop the cherry" mean?

"Cherry" is a slang term referring to the opening of the vagina. "Pop the cherry" refers to the breaking of the maidenhead or hymen the first time a woman has intercourse, although often it is broken long before. See below.

This term probably caught on because when the maidenhead or hymen is broken the first time a woman has sexual intercourse, there may be a small amount of bleeding, so the opening looks red like a cherry.

62 What is a virgin? What is losing your virginity?

A virgin is someone who has never had sexual intercourse. In men, there is no physical difference to the penis "before" and "after," but in a woman there is a thin piece of skin covering the opening of the vagina, called the hymen. Traditionally, this skin was thought to be broken the first time a woman had intercourse, and so when it was broken, it was assumed that the woman was no longer a virgin. But this is more folktale than truth. For many girls, the hymen is gone by the time she first has sex. It may have been broken or stretched during sports or exercise before the girl ever had any kind of sexual experience.

However, if a woman has never had intercourse before, it is important for both the man and woman to know about the hymen. The woman may choose to have her medical doctor break it painlessly, using a local anaesthetic, before her first sexual experience, so that her first experience of sexual intercourse is not painful. Or the woman can realize that some discomfort and bleeding after her first experience with sexual intercourse is due to the breaking of the hymen.

63 What is the clitoris?

The clitoris is the center for sexual pleasure and orgasm in women. It is located between the lips or labia, which cover the area of the sexual organs, just above the vaginal opening.

64 Can a woman "come" more than once?

"Come" is a slang term for having an orgasm. Yes, most women can have several orgasms fairly close together. Often, her partner's stimulation of the clitoris can help her have an orgasm.

F. MENSTRUATION AND THE MENSTRUAL CYCLE

65 Where is the egg or ovum made in the female? At what age does she begin to produce eggs?

Strictly speaking, the woman does not **make ova** (eggs) at all. She is born with all the ova she will ever have. They are all stored in the two ovaries.

As a girl begins to mature into a woman, as early as nine years of age, but usually between ages ten and twelve years, the eggs begin to ripen. Usually one egg ripens each month, because the ovaries are stimulated by certain hormonal chemicals in her blood.

When the egg has matured sufficiently, it leaves the ovary and enters the **fallopian tubes.** There, if it encounters a sperm, it becomes fertilized, moves into the uterus and a new baby begins to grow. The woman has become pregnant. If the egg is not fertilized, it leaves the body during menstruation. See the section on pregnancy and childbirth for more information.

66 What is a period or menstruation? Why do girls menstruate?

Every month, a woman's body prepares itself to become pregnant and to nurture a fertilized egg in the uterus for nine months until it has grown into a fully developed baby, and is ready to be born. As part of this preparation, each month the lining of the uterus becomes rich with nutrients intended to nourish the new baby.

Menstruation occurs if the woman does not become pregnant. Then, the uterus discharges the lining, along with a small amount of blood, that it no longer needs. It comes out through the vagina. The average length of a menstrual period is about five days. It normally doesn't hurt.

A young woman needs to wear some kind of pad to absorb the trickle of blood. All young women have periods, from puberty until their late forties or early fifties. They quickly become used to them, and find that they can do most everything during their periods that they do the rest of the time. It is not a sickness or weak condition.

67 What is the average age at which menstruation begins?

Some girls start as early as eight or nine, others not until they are sixteen. The average age is ten to twelve. It is often the case that a girl will start about the same time as her mother did, so you may get a rough idea by asking your mother. It doesn't mean that you are less of a woman if you start later than others. Each individual has her own timetable of development, but by about sixteen or seventeen it all evens out.

If, by the age of sixteen years a young woman has not started her period, she should discuss it with her doctor.

68 Do boys have menstrual periods?

No. Only girls and women menstruate, because they prepare for pregnancy each month. Only girls and women need to dispose of unfertilized eggs and the unused lining of the uterus once a month. Boys and men of course do not have uteruses and do not produce eggs.

69 What happens if the girl does not menstruate on time? Does the lining just stay inside? Can it hurt her?

A girl cannot die or become ill from not menstruating. But if she does not start having periods by about the age of sixteen years, she should consult a doctor.

70 Do you ever stop having menstrual periods? Does a woman ever stop producing ripe eggs? What is meant by "change of life?"

Yes. Most women stop menstruating around the time they are anywhere from thirty-eight to fifty years of age. Some stop as early as the age of thirty-five years, some stop later than fifty-five years of age.

Periods stop during the change of life called **menopause.** During this time, a woman stops ripening and releasing eggs for fertilization, and her body experiences other changes. This time of change lasts two to three years. When this change occurs, a woman is no longer able to bear children.

However, in all other respects women remain healthy, vigorous and active long after menopause. A woman is not "over the hill" after this time.

71 Can I do such active things as play basketball, swim, take a bath or shampoo my hair while I am menstruating?

You certainly can. In fact, it is a good idea to stay active and exercise during this time. Of course, if you get tired, you will realize that you have overdone it, but usually the more active you are, the better you will feel. Having your period does not mean you are sick; it is a normal occurrence that all women experience. It can be a little inconvenient, but before long you will get used to it and hardly think about it.

In a public pool, you may need to use a tampon while menstruating. However, if you are swimming in a lake for a short time, a pad or tampon may not be necessary. Using common sense about swimming and other forms of exercise is a good idea whether you are having your period or not.

It is important to take frequent baths or showers during your period. Not only is this important to keep your sexual organs clean, but then you won't have to worry that you might have some odor. The body odor results from increased oil production from glands which take place during the teen years.

72 Why do some girls get moody just before or when they start their periods?

A woman experiences a change in the chemicals—the hormones—in her body, just as she is about to have her period. This often affects her mood. She may feel a little low or "blue" for a few days.

This is a time to be especially careful not to pick a fight with your close friends. If you are a woman who has such a mood change, you need to learn to be ready for it. You need to learn to manage them so that you don't create bad feelings between you and your friends and teachers that you will later regret. It is also a good idea not to make any decisions about something important to you if you start to feel discouraged. In a few days, you will be over it. Just being aware that this mood change is happening may make it less hard on you.

Of course many girls and women don't experience such mood swings. This is also normal—they are just luckier than the rest of us.

73 What happens if one of the eggs breaks? Can it injure the woman?

No. The eggs are very tiny—only about the size of the head of a pin. They do not have hard shells like bird eggs. If something happens to one, the body silently and naturally disposes of it, just as it does with the thousands of other body cells that die every day. The woman never even knows anything has happened.

74 If a girl's body changes each month when she is as young as nine or ten, doesn't this mean she is ready to have a baby then?

Let's distinguish between two things: the **physical ability** to do something and the **emotional maturity** to do something. A nine year old child could probably learn how to drive a car; she is physically capable of doing it. But she is probably not emotionally mature enough to do it. If she sees someone she likes, she might forget to look at the road. Or, if another car cuts in front of her, she might lose her temper and smash her car into it.

The same is true for having a child. A boy can become a father, a girl a mother, even as young as nine or ten. The girl's body starts to prepare each month for pregnancy at about this time. The body does not know whether the girl or boy is emotionally ready to take on the responsibility of a child.

Long ago, when people lived in large family groups, and many children died young, it made more sense for girls in their early teens to start having babies. That way, they could have as many babies as possible, making it more likely that some would survive to grow up. Then, the older family members were there to take care of them. But nowadays, when parents are expected to take care of their own children, it makes no sense for young teenagers to have children. They are not emotionally ready to take care of a baby. They are still children themselves. They don't want to spend many hours each day caring for the baby's every need. They don't have jobs that will provide money to support the baby. They may find that they only had a "crush" on each other and do not want to stay together. Then the child will have only one full-time parent, if that.

75 How long does a menstrual period last? Why do some girls have longer periods than others?

A menstrual period may last about three to five days. But some may last for a week or more, and there may seem to be a larger amount of blood lost. However, the total amount is only about one-quarter cup. Each girl is different in how she matures. Some girls have regular periods; some do not.[4]

76 How often can I expect to have my periods?

On average, every twenty-eight days—slightly more often than once per month. But some women may have them a little more often, some only once every two to three months. They will continue for about five days each month until you are perhaps fifty years of age. They will cease temporarily during pregnancy.

77 Why do women miss periods? Why did I have two periods in one month, and then no period the next month?

It may take as long as two years before some girls' periods come regularly, while others may be regular from the start. Menstruation is switched on and off by two chemicals, estrogen and progestoren. At first a girl may not have enough of these chemicals to switch them on and off on a regular schedule. Frequent or irregular periods are nothing to worry about when you are just starting out. A continuous, heavy flow longer than a week requires immediate medical attention.

An occasional missed period is nothing to worry about either, especially if a girl is just starting her periods. Once a woman starts menstruating regularly, if she does not have a period for two months or more, she should consult a doctor. The most common reason for this is that she has become pregnant. Her body has changed over to providing nourishment for the embryo and growing fetus, so her menstrual periods stop during pregnancy.

If a woman is not pregnant, she may have some medical problem that the doctor can treat. Continued strenuous exercise can also stop menstruation, as can a skimpy or inadequate diet. When a woman gets to be fifty or so, she stops menstruating. This is called menopause.

Some women's periods are never regular. But this is only an inconvenience, about as annoying as getting sun-burned very easily. They get pregnant and have children just the same, even though they are not on a precise schedule.

78 My period is late. Does that mean I'm pregnant?

A girl can only become pregnant through sexual intercourse — that is, by a boy or man inserting his penis into her vagina, or having it near the outside of her vagina. If you have never done these things, you cannot become pregnant. Often a girl can be late or miss a period without anything being the matter. Sometimes worry, tiredness or unusually strenuous exercise can cause this to happen. During the first year, you may not have regular periods.

Only if you miss two in a row — or you have recently had intercourse and have good reason to think you may be pregnant — should you worry. Then, you should consult a medical doctor immediately. If you are pregnant, you may need to talk to your parents, the father, trusted

friends or teachers, a school counsellor or minister about what you are
going to do.

79 What is "spotting?"

Soon after they begin to menstruate, some girls have what seems like a
light period for several weeks. This is called spotting. Often spotting
clears up by itself, as your body's menstrual cycle becomes more regular.
If spotting happens to you and it lasts more than three months, speak to a
doctor or nurse-practitioner about it, or ask your mother to speak to one.
It is usually not a real medical problem, but it is annoying to have to
wear a pad or tampon all the time, and the doctor can give medication
that will make your period regular.

80 What happens if I never have a period?

If you have not had one by the time you are sixteen years old, you
should speak to your doctor. The doctor may suggest that you wait
another year, or prescribe medicines for you that contain the chemicals—
the hormones—that your body normally produces itself to start you
menstruating. Sometimes your body needs this medicine to prod it to get
going, but then keeps going by itself.

If a woman never has a period, this probably means that she can't have
babies, but very, very few women never have periods. Some women have
only two or three per year.

81 How can I tell when I am about to have my period? What happens if it starts while I am in school or out with my friends?

Sometimes you may feel a backache or stomach cramps just before
your period. Often, the first sign may be a pink or brown spot on your
sheets or nightgown. Or you may notice a spot on your underwear when
you go to the bathroom. Sometimes, you may feel a wet feeling between
your legs.

The flow is very small at first, so you have an hour or two before it will
come through your outer clothing, and you have some time to obtain a
pad. If you think you are going to start soon, it is a very good idea to start
keeping pads in your locker, desk or in a paper bag, or tampons in your
purse.

If you get stuck in school without a pad, ask a teacher or the school
nurse for one. If your teacher is a man and you need to leave your class,
you don't need to say exactly why—just say you need to go to the

bathroom, that you feel sick or that it is an emergency. You might check ahead with a (woman) teacher or secretary you know to find out the procedure in your school.[5]

At first, your periods may not be very regular, but after awhile they will become regular. You can figure out when your periods can be expected by marking on a calendar when each period begins and ends. After several months, you will have a good idea of what to expect.

82 Why do I get cramps during my period? What can I do about them?

The menstrual blood comes from the uterus. This organ is very muscular, and sometimes the muscles contract or twitch. This can feel like back or stomach pains.

No girl needs to put up with painful cramps. Extra exercise can help a great deal. Try riding a bicycle or just walking, to limber up your body's muscles. You can also try a warm bath, or placing a hot pad on your stomach or back, depending on where you feel them. Be sure to get plenty of sleep and not allow yourself to get very tired. Also eat more protein all month. Your mother may have some helpful suggestions too.

You can also take aspirin, acetominophen (Tylenol is the most well-known brand), ibuprofen, or if these don't work, special menstrual pills. You may need two, but it is better to start with one than to take too many, even though these are all available without a prescription. If you have recurrent cramps it is wise to ask your doctor for advice.

83 What does a woman use to catch the menstrual blood?

There are two different general types of products. One is the pad or sanitary napkin that she wears inside her underpants. It can be held on either by a belt or by adhesives that attach it to the inside of the underpants. These can be changed as often as necessary.

The other is the tampon. This is a small piece of absorbent material that is inserted into the vagina, and must be changed several times per day.

All the types of pads come in various shapes and thicknesses. You should try them all until you find the one with which you are most comfortable and feel the most safe and secure. You might try a different type every month, to find the one you like best.

84 Can anyone tell if you have a pad on?

No. Of course you can feel the pad or sanitary napkin yourself, but it fits between your legs, and it doesn't make a bulge in your clothing. There are several kinds of pads; you should try them all until you find the one with which you are most comfortable.

As long as you shower every day, especially washing the vaginal opening, and change your pad two or three times a day, there will not be any odor. The menstrual blood only begins to have an odor after it has been on the pad for several hours or has dried on your body.

If you think someone else is having her period, you are probably wrong! In any case, it is a good idea not to mention it unless she does first. This is a very private matter. It is especially hurtful to tease someone about her period.

85 What is a tampon?

A tampon is a piece of cotton that has been made into a small plug. This plug is placed up inside the vagina. It catches the menstrual flow before it leaves the body. A small string hangs out so that the tampon can be taken out easily and painlessly. Many women prefer the convenience of this kind of protection.

During the day you should change a tampon often, every three to four hours. New super tampons may be left in longer, but you must be very careful not to leave them in longer than the instructions allow. Leaving one in too long can cause an infection, especially one very serious kind of infection called toxic shock syndrome that may kill in a short time. But if you do not use one for more than the proper amount of time, you don't have to worry.

86 Should I be a certain age before I start using tampons? Does it hurt to put a tampon in?

There is no particular age to wear tampons. Normally, inserting a tampon does not hurt and wearing a tampon is completely painless and comfortable. You do not have to wait until you have had sexual intercourse.

Remember to tilt the tampon toward the small of the back, as the vagina itself is tilted in this direction. Also, many women don't realize that they have to push the tampon in as far as it will go. If it is not in all the way, it can feel very uncomfortable.

Sometimes, when a girl is just beginning to menstruate, her vagina has not grown large enough to allow for the comfortable insertion of a tampon. If it hurts to put it in or is uncomfortable, you can try junior tampons. If even these are uncomfortable, you probably need to wait until you grow a little bit more.

If you have been wearing tampons and they suddenly start to hurt, or if you are full grown and they still hurt, you should consult a doctor right away.

87 Has a tampon ever become stuck? What happens if the string comes off?

Many young women worry about this, and I suppose that anything is possible, but I have never heard of the tampon becoming stuck or the string breaking off. In my classes, I sometimes keep one tampon all term and pull on the string in every class. It has never come off yet!

Even if the string did come off, you can just reach in and pull the tampon out. The vagina is only three to five inches long, so the tampon is not out of reach.

88 Can I use tampons if I am still a virgin? Will the tampon break the maidenhead (hymen)?

Yes you can. If the hymen or maidenhead is not broken for some other reason, it can stretch enough to allow a tampon to be inserted, without breaking.

89 How do you go to the bathroom with a pad on?

There are three basic kinds of pads. One kind is fastened to a small belt that goes around your waist. This can be slipped down to allow you to go to the bathroom. The second kind sticks to your underpants. When you pull your underpants down, you also pull the pad down. The third is called a tampon. It fits inside the vagina, and usually has a string attached to it to make it easy to remove. But it does not have to be removed to go to the bathroom. However, often girls change to a fresh pad at the same time that they go to the bathroom. Follow the disposal instructions on the package (see Question 91).

90 Once you start to menstruate, do you always have to wear a pad?

A woman always has to wear some kind of protection during her period. Although only a small amount of blood trickles out—about a quarter of a cup—a pad or tampon is necessary to prevent her clothes, bedsheets and blankets from being stained.

91 If your flow during your period is heavy, how do you urinate?

The blood flow of your period does not come from the same opening as the one from which you urinate. These openings are not connected to each other, and so your period won't interfere with urinating.

If you are wearing a pad, you will need to remove it temporarily while you go to the bathroom. However, if you are using a tampon, you can leave it in. Some women prefer to change pads or tampons when they go to the bathroom, but this isn't necessary unless the pad needs changing anyway.

92 What is the white substance that sometimes comes out of my vagina? Is it normal to have this discharge right before or right after my period?

This whitish discharge is a normal discharge from your vagina. The vagina has watery liquid in it something like the saliva in the mouth. It keeps the vagina clean and moist. At some times of your menstrual cycle there is more of this liquid than at others. When there is a lot, some of it may trickle out. Then, you may notice a whitish discharge. It dries quickly and doesn't cause embarrassing odors.

However, you need to be concerned if the color changes or becomes heavier than usual. A discharge with a yellowish or greenish color, or an odor, or that seems different in some other way, may indicate an infection. A vaginal itch or sting also may mean that you have an infection. Then you should consult your doctor or go to a clinic. Do not try to get rid of it yourself. Such infections are usually easy to cure, but only a doctor can treat them properly. If you don't have an infection cured, it may cause serious problems and may even prevent you from having children later.

There is nothing shameful about having a vaginal infection. Some women have them often, some occasionally, some never. We often don't know what causes them. It is no disgrace and doesn't "prove" that you have been engaging in sexual activity. It is just uncomfortable. A doctor should treat it as soon as possible.

93 What is a hysterectomy? What is a "D and C?"

A hysterectomy is a major surgical operation in which the uterus is removed. After this operation, the woman can no longer have children, and she no longer has menstrual periods. If you or someone you know has been told to have a hysterectomy, the person involved should consult one or more additional doctors for a second and even third opinion.

A hysterectomy can be necessary for a variety of reasons. If a problem cannot be corrected by medication, the doctor may recommend a hysterectomy.

A less drastic operation is the dilation and curetage, or "D and C." This operation involves dilating, or widening the opening in the cervix and scraping the lining of the uterus. Often this is all that is needed to restore the uterus to its proper functioning.

94 What is breast cancer? How do you know if you have it?

One-fifth of all cancer in women is breast cancer. Cancer occurs when the cells in some part of the body become abnormal and begin reproducing rapidly. After a time, they invade the blood stream and lymphatic system, traveling to other parts of the body. If the breast cancer is caught early it is almost always curable.

Breast cancer can spread rapidly so it is important for a woman to examine her breasts regularly and, when she reaches the age of thirty-five years (or around thirty years if there is a history of breast cancer in her family), to begin regular mammograms at least once a year. Self breast examinations are fairly easy to do and effective in detecting changes in a woman's breasts. If you see any unusual change in your breasts, consult your doctor at once.

A mammogram is basically an x-ray of a woman's breast tissue. An x-ray machine designed specifically to perform mammograms is used and operated by a female radiology technician. Mammograms often detect potential tumors as small as the head of a pin and other changes; this early detection helps in the increased cure rate for breast cancer. The procedure is painless and takes only a little time.

There are several types of treatment for breast cancer; not all of them involve radical surgery. It is a good idea to get a second, or even third, opinion about whatever treatment is suggested. Just as with other forms of cancer, it is rare for a teenaged girl to develop breast cancer.

After a woman is sixteen years old, she should begin having both a pap smear and breast examination by her doctor once a year. A pap smear is a process where the doctor scrapes tissue samples from the cervix, which is located at the top of the vagina. This tissue is sent to a laboratory where the cells are checked for abnormalities. This test helps to warn of cervical and uterine cancer years before the cancer begins to form.

REFERENCES

1. Bell, Ruth. *Changing Bodies Changing Lives.* New York: Random House, 1980, p. 5.
2. Calderone, M. and Johnson, E. *Family Book of Sexuality.* New York: Bantam Books, 1983, pp. 38–43.
3. Kelly, G. F. *Sexuality: The Human Perspective.* New York: Barron's Educational Series, Inc., 1980, pp. 23–24.
4. Boston Women's Health Book Collective. *Our Bodies Ourselves.* New York: Simon and Schuster, 1976, p. 34.
5. Ibid, pp. 32–33.

Chapter II

CONCEPTION, PREGNANCY AND CHILDBIRTH

A. CONCEPTION AND PREGNANCY

1 Where was I before I was born? How did I begin?

You started out first as a tiny cell inside your mother's body. This cell had instructions from both your mother and father, called genes and chromosomes, that told it how to grow into you. This cell divided into two cells, and each of these cells divided again. This process of division continued throughout your development, and is continuing now at a slower rate. Each new cell contained the exact same genes and chromosomes with the exact same instructions as the first cell. These cells became specialized: some became nerve cells, some became muscle cells, some became skin cells. Your brain and nerves were formed by nerve cells, your heart and body muscles were formed from muscle cells, and your skin was formed from skin cells. After three months of this dividing, there were many millions of cells, and you started to look like a baby. There is disagreement about exactly when a growing fetus is considered a human being.

2 Why does a baby chick come from an egg?

Chickens and other birds, fish, snakes and other reptiles, frogs and toads and other amphibians, do not keep their babies inside them until the babies can live on their own the way people do. Instead, they lay eggs. A male chicken or rooster must have intercourse with the female chicken to fertilize the egg, but the egg does not stay inside the mother until the young chick is ready to be born. After fertilization, the female chicken lays the egg and then sits on it to give the growing chick the proper warmth that it needs to grow. The egg has a hard shell that protects the chick.

3 Why do I have a bellybutton?

When you were a tiny baby growing inside of your mother's uterus, you couldn't eat or breath for yourself. There was a tube connecting you to your mother's body called the umbilical cord. It was attached at your navel, or "belly button." The food, water and oxygen that you needed to live on went through the tube from your mother to you. Also, waste products from your body went from you to your mother's body, which

45

could dispose of them. After you were born, you no longer needed the umbilical cord. As soon as you were born, someone—usually a doctor— cut the cord. This was painless for both you and your mother. After a few weeks, the place where the cord was attached healed up, and became your navel.

Inside the woman's uterus is a special organ called the **placenta**, where the oxygen and nutrients from your mother are transferred to the baby.

4 Does a baby grow inside its mother's stomach?

No. The baby grows inside a special, protective place called the uterus or womb. From the outside, the baby may look like it is in the mother's stomach because as it grows, it fills up the space where the stomach usually is, and pushes the stomach out of the way.

5 How does a new baby get started? What is fertilization and where does it occur?

The male and female sexual organs each have their roles to play in creating a new person. The man's testicles, located just below and behind his penis, produce sperm by the millions. During ejaculation the sperm leave the testicles, travel into the body along the vas deferens and through the prostate gland. This gland adds fluid to the sperm to help carry them along and keep them alive. Then the sperm and fluid, called semen, travel through the penis and out. If ejaculation occurs during sexual intercourse with a woman, the sperm are placed in the woman's vagina and travel upward in search of an egg to fertilize.

The sperm go from the vagina through the cervix to the uterus. They proceed upward through the uterus to one of two **fallopian tubes.** At the other end of these tubes are the ovaries. The ovaries ripen and release the eggs or **ova,** usually one per month. It is in these tubes—between the uterus and the ovaries—that the sperm meet up with the egg and one sperm enters the egg. When it enters, fertilization takes place. Then the fertilized egg travels back down the fallopian tube into the uterus. It settles into the lining of the uterus where the baby develops. After nine months, the baby has grown enough to leave the mother's body. Then it is born by traveling down and out of the uterus, through the vagina to the outside world. This is why the vaginal tube is often called the birth canal.

If the egg is not fertilized, it and the uterine lining (made up of tissue and a small amount of blood) are discharged through the vagina during menstruation.

6 How do sperm find and enter the egg? Why can't more than one sperm enter?

Each sperm has a tail which swings rapidly back and forth, driving it forward. A sperm cell can live for about 48 hours inside the woman's body —long enough for it to propel itself upward against the force of gravity, through the uterus and into the fallopian tubes. There, if it encounters an egg, a chemical in its head creates an opening in the egg's outer wall. The first sperm to penetrate this wall is drawn into the center of the egg, where fertilization takes place. Once this first sperm cell has entered, the egg cell's outer wall becomes impenetrable to all other sperm.

7 What happens to all the sperm that don't fertilize an egg?

The sperm can live up to forty eight hours inside a woman's body. Those that do not fertilize an egg—nearly all of them—simply die and are absorbed by the woman's body. Thousands of our body cells die every day, and are collected by the body, broken down and given off along with other waste products. The sperm cells are disposed of in the same way.

8 Can a girl get pregnant from kissing?

No, she cannot. The only sexual activity that can cause pregnancy is sexual intercourse or near-intercourse, in which the male's sperm is deposited in or near the female's vagina.

9 At what age can a boy become a father?

Usually a boy can first become a father any time after his tenth birthday. For some boys it is earlier, for others later. A boy can tell by whether he has ever ejaculated semen, a white, thick fluid, from his penis—perhaps during a "wet dream." This ejaculation may contain sperm that could begin a pregnancy should they be combined with an ovum or egg from a female (not all ejaculate may contain sperm in young boys).

10 At what age can a girl become a mother? Can you get pregnant without ever having menstruated?

A woman can first become pregnant some time between her ninth and sixteenth birthdays. The youngest girl I know of to have a baby was ten years old. A girl who has not yet menstruated can still become pregnant. A girl will first **know** that she may become pregnant by her first menstrual period, but she may become pregnant before then. Sometimes a boy may tell a girl that it is safe to have sex with him because she has not yet menstruated. This is wrong! It is not menstruation that makes a girl able to have children, but rather the presence of a ripe egg (ovum) in one of her fallopian tubes. Even a nine-year-old girl can have a mature ovum inside her body, although she has not yet menstruated. This is important to understand, because nine years old is far too young to have a child.

11 Does pregnancy harm a girl? What are some of the health problems with teen pregnancy?

Pregnancy is a normal process in a healthy adult woman and usually does not harm her. However, a young girl's body is not yet fully developed, and so pregnancy can put a real strain on it. This strain can create health problems which sometimes plague her for the rest of her life. Pregnancy can be especially hard on a teenage girl's kidneys and bladder, the organs involved in eliminating the body's waste products in the form of urine. The kidneys are working for both the mother and the baby, and excess strain may damage them so that they continue to have problems for the rest of the mother's life. The growing fetus also needs lots of calcium. If the girl isn't eating enough, the calcium may come from her own bones and teeth to be used for her baby. She may have problems with her teeth or arthritis in later years because her body gave this calcium to the baby.

Babies born to teen mothers also have many more health problems than babies born to adult women.[1]

12 How old should you be before you have a child?

The best time to have a baby is between eighteen and thirty-five to forty years of age. Before age eighteen and after age thirty-five years, there is more risk to the health of both mother and fetus. Women below this age have not yet finished their own growth, and women over the age of thirty-five years run an increasing risk of having a baby with birth defects. Older women may not be as able as younger women to withstand the strain of childbearing. However, many older women who have postponed childbearing for any number of reasons are having healthy babies into their forties. Women now get more exercise and stay in top physical condition much longer than they used to.

13 How old does a girl have to be to have a baby?

This is really two questions in one: at what age does a girl become able to have a baby, and at what age is it best to begin having children?

Little girls have the organs that they need to have babies—a vagina where the baby comes out, a uterus and ovaries. But they are not yet in "working order" to enable the girl to become pregnant. At about the age of nine or ten the girl's body may release an egg that could develop into a baby. If she were to have intercourse with a boy who is producing sperm, she might get pregnant even at this young age. The youngest mother I know of gave birth at age ten in a hospital in the city where I live.

But a girl this age is much too young to get pregnant. Her body is not yet fully developed, and it is likely that the baby will have serious health problems while it is developing inside the mother or after it is born. Even if the baby develops normally, a girl this age cannot support herself and certainly is not ready to take care of the child. Even at sixteen or seventeen years of age, most girls are not ready to take care of a young child by themselves. Caring for a young child is something parents do all day, every day—it takes much more time than a "full-time" job. It is **much** better for both the mother and child for the woman to wait until she has finished school, has married and has adequate income for the whole family to live comfortably.

But it is important for girls who are only nine years old to understand that they can become pregnant, and to say no to any boy or man who wants to place his penis inside the girl's vagina (have intercourse).

14 When can't a woman get pregnant?

A woman can't get pregnant when she is a very young girl, less than about nine years of age, since her eggs have not yet begun to ripen. She cannot start a new baby when she is already pregnant, as her body stops the egg-ripening process once a baby is conceived. She cannot get pregnant after she has stopped menstruating—menopause—because she is no longer ripening eggs.

For women who are menstruating, there are times in the monthly cycle when she has no ripe or fertile eggs. She may be able to tell when these are or she may not. Since the menstrual cycle usually is not exactly one month long, this time of infertility does not occur at the same time each month. Especially if she is a teenager and her periods are still irregular, it will be very difficult for her to tell where she is in her menstrual cycle. It is better to use some form of birth control (contraception), unless her religious beliefs make this impossible.

It was once believed that a woman could not become pregnant when she was menstruating or nursing her baby. We now know this is not true of all women. Some women do become pregnant during these times.

15 Can a woman become pregnant from sperm on a toilet seat, or from sperm in a bathtub or swimming pool?

No. The sperm need to remain in the fluid, called semen, which carries them out of the man's penis, and they need to remain at body temperature to stay alive. You can't get pregnant from sperm left on a bed sheet either, because semen exposed to the open air dries very quickly, and the sperm cannot live without it.

16 Can a girl get pregnant if she is still a virgin or if she just "fools around" and doesn't have intercourse?

Most teenagers know that a baby begins after sexual intercourse, but they don't realize it can also happen without intercourse. If a man places his erect penis near a woman's vagina, sperm can be left outside it. They can survive long enough in the warm, moist environment to enter the vagina, find an egg and fertilize it, and so begin a baby. Even if the boy doesn't ejaculate, some sperm can come out. We call women who get pregnant in this way "pregnant virgins." Even a tiny drop of semen can contain a million or more sperm. One sperm cell is enough to begin a new baby.

A woman can also be impregnated by a doctor who places a man's sperm inside the woman's vagina. This is called artificial insemination. It is usually done because there is some medical condition that prevents the couple from conceiving a child in the normal way.[2]

17 Can a girl get pregnant if the boy "pulls out" before he ejaculates?

Yes. When a boy is highly aroused sexually, there is a thin secretion from his penis that contains some sperm even if he has not ejaculated. Remember, it only takes one sperm for a girl to become pregnant.

Also, sometimes the boy doesn't pull out in time. Remember, at that moment, there is a very strong desire **not** to pull out!

18 Can you get pregnant the first time you have intercourse?

You certainly can, and it is just as likely as any other time you have sex. Don't kid yourself that you or your partner are somehow specially protected the first time!

19 Do you get pregnant every time you have sexual intercourse?

No. Every woman is different. Women can become pregnant at any time during their monthly cycle—they are more likely to become pregnant immediately after ovulation. However, it is not always easy to tell just when ovulation occurs, so having intercourse without contraception always runs the risk of pregnancy.

20 If a woman has unprotected sexual intercourse, how long does it take for the sperm to reach the egg? Where is the egg at this time?

To reach the egg, the sperm must enter the vagina, travel up and through the cervix into the uterus, travel through it to one of the fallopian tubes, then travel up the tube until it encounters an egg. It only takes a few minutes for the sperm to travel from the vagina into the uterus, but it takes them several hours to travel through the uterus and up a fallopian tube to an egg. Although the total journey is only a few inches, the sperm are extremely tiny, and must struggle against gravity. The woman cannot feel the moment of fertilization. The egg, after it is released from the ovary, passes into the fallopian tube where it can be fertilized if sperm are present.

21 What are the odds of getting pregnant each time a teenage woman has intercourse? Suppose I have been doing it regularly for awhile and have not become pregnant—am I safe?

It's very hard to come up with a number. But teenage women are usually very fertile—they easily become pregnant. Don't kid yourself by saying, "This couldn't happen to me" or saying "It hasn't happened so far; it must be safe to have intercourse." It is **never safe** for a teenaged girl to have unprotected sex. Every teenaged girl and woman has an ovulation period each month when she has an egg in her fallopian tube and can become pregnant.

If you must have intercourse, it is much better to use a reliable form of birth control (contraception). (See the chapter on contraception.) Even the best form of birth control doesn't always work, but it will greatly improve your chances of not getting pregnant.

22 How many teenage girls get pregnant each year? Do teenagers have more babies than older women?

Even one unwanted teen pregnancy is one too many. This country is the eighth highest in teen pregnancies among the thirty advanced countries for which such information is available. Numbers change each year but reliable estimates state that one out of ten teenaged girls become pregnant. Most of these pregnancies are not intended. Over 1.3 million children are living with teenaged mothers—half of these mothers are unmarried.[3]

23 How can I tell if I am pregnant?

The first sign is usually a missed period. If you have had intercourse since your last period, and you do not menstruate, you may be pregnant. However, if you have recently begun menstruating and your period is still irregular, you may not be able to tell right away. Or, if you have not yet begun to menstruate you may not realize you are pregnant until several months later, when you notice you are putting on weight. Also, some women have a small discharge of blood that looks like a period even after becoming pregnant, and so may not realize it until their second period is missed.

Another sign of pregnancy is the darkening of the area of the nipples of the breasts. Also, the breasts themselves will gradually enlarge. Still another sign is a "thickening" of the waistline, that makes the woman look as though she has gained about ten pounds.

24 What do they do to you when you have a pregnancy test? Do the home pregnancy test kits really work?

A doctor or family planning clinic can quickly administer a completely painless pregnancy test. All they need is a sample of the woman's urine usually two weeks after the menstrual period. The results are available in only a few minutes. You can ask them whether they keep the results strictly confidential—most clinics and doctors do for minors as well as adults.

There are now also reliable and inexpensive self-test kits that need a few drops of the woman's urine. They are available in drug stores to enable a woman to find out if she is pregnant. These are becoming simpler to use than they were when they first came out. A woman who follows the instructions carefully will know the results in less than an hour.

But a woman who is not absolutely sure she has done the home test correctly, is better off going to a doctor or family planning clinic, where the tests are quite reliable. And, since a pregnant woman should be under regular prenatal care, it is simply a good idea to see a doctor or nurse-practitioner when you first suspect you may be pregnant.

25 I think I am pregnant, but I'm too scared to find out. What should I do?

If you think you are pregnant, it's only natural to be scared, but don't let your fear paralyze you. Letting your fears overwhelm you may be the worst part of the whole situation. Try to take things one step at a time. It is very important that you go to a family planning clinic or your doctor right away to find out whether you are pregnant or not. You can bring a friend with you. Although the people at most clinics will treat you courteously, bringing someone you know who cares about you will make it easier. Even if you learn you are not pregnant, the clinic is a good place to find out about birth control so that you won't have another scare.

If you find out that you are pregnant, talk over your situation with your parents if you are able to, or with trusted friends, teachers, a school counsellor, minister or doctor.

If you don't know a doctor whom you trust, the family planning clinic will help you to find one. It will also provide you with trained counsellors who will discuss the options with you: having the baby and giving it up for adoption, having the baby and keeping it or having an abortion. The counsellors will also help you discuss the situation with your parents and the father of the baby, and suggest other social service and religious agencies that can help you in various ways.

These agencies should not pressure you into making one choice or another, and if they do, you should look elsewhere. Some anti-abortion groups masquerade as supportive family planning clinics, but they have already decided to tell you what you should do before you walk in the door.

If you decide to have the baby, it is important to get good health care very early in the pregnancy. Teenage girls need to be sure of having proper nutrition and being in the best of health, to give the fetus the best possible chance of growing into a healthy baby.

26 A girl I have been having sex with says she is pregnant. What should I do?

You can let her know that you will stick with her and help her as best you can. You can begin by accompanying her to the family planning clinic or doctor for a pregnancy test. They will provide both of you with counselling, and help you both to discuss the situation with your parents.

Don't try to impose your choice on her for what you think she should do. This is her decision to make, and she will have to find the strength in herself to decide whether to keep the baby to raise herself. Your concern and support will make these tremendously difficult decisions less overwhelming for both of you.

27 How long after I become pregnant can I find out about it?

For a urine test, you must wait four to six weeks after intercourse—two weeks after a missed period for a pregnancy test. Some tests can be used within two weeks after conception. If there is some reason that you need to know more quickly, a doctor or medical laboratory can perform a blood test as soon as two days after you have had intercourse. This test is more expensive.

28 What should a teenage girl who is pregnant do? Should she keep the baby, give it up for adoption or have an abortion?

Whether to keep the baby, give it up for adoption or not have it at all are very difficult decisions, and I can't possibly tell you what the best decision is for you. The question of abortion particularly depends on your religious and moral beliefs. Some people think that even a one-month-old fetus is already a complete human being, and therefore that abortion is terribly wrong. Others say that it cannot think, is not yet aware of anything and that it is better for a child to be born to adult parents who are ready, willing and able to take care of it.

Whether to keep or give up the baby once it is born is also not easy to decide. Many teenage girls now are keeping their babies. At first they think they can work out all the problems of caring for it. Often their friends and families pressure them to keep it. A girl's parents may like the idea of being grandparents.

But all too often, two or three years later, the girl finds that it is much more difficult than she anticipated. She may have found that she can't live decently without working, and has no one to help care for the child. Or she may have found a man she wants to marry, but who doesn't want someone else's child. She may feel that the child isn't really hers, because her parents have taken over raising it.

Then she may give up the child. But it is much harder for a two- or three-year-old to find permanent parents than for a newborn, and it may be shifted from one foster home to another. It is also much harder for the child who has become attached to its mother to experience this separation.

In choosing adoption, nowadays a mother can have some say over which family adopts her child. She may be able to know something of who they are, what they do, although it still may be difficult for her to actually meet the adoptive parents.

Before you make a decision, be sure and talk it over with several mature adults whom you trust and who are more neutral and not directly involved in your life.

29 What is an abortion? Is abortion a safe procedure?

An abortion is the termination of a pregnancy before the fetus is capable of surviving on its own. There are two types of abortion: a spontaneous abortion and a voluntary abortion. The first, also called a miscarriage, is discussed more fully below, in Question 43.

In a voluntary abortion, the woman decides to end the pregnancy. This may be because she has been raped, because the pregnancy is threatening her own life or because she feels that she is not ready or able to properly care for a baby. Abortions must be performed by doctors in appropriate clinics or hospitals.

In the first three months of pregnancy, the procedure is technically fairly simple. Later on, more difficult procedures must be used that are more risky to the mother. However **medically** simple abortion is, it is not so **emotionally** simple, and may cause serious emotional upset. It is much better to use good contraception or avoid intercourse, rather than thinking that an abortion is "no big deal."

30 How long after a baby is conceived can the mother still have a legal abortion?

An abortion performed after 12 weeks is more dangerous to the mother. Abortion laws vary from state to state, with some limiting abortion to twenty weeks, others allowing abortions up to twenty-four weeks.

Often people do not realize that the decision of whether or not to have an abortion needs to be made as soon as possible after the woman learns she is pregnant.

Deciding to have an abortion is a very difficult decision. You need to talk it over with mature adults whom you trust—if you can't discuss it with your parents, try to find an understanding school counsellor, minister, doctor or other adult friend to discuss it with. The more adult opinions you hear, the more likely it is that you will make the decision that is best **for you.** Even though it may seem easier to take the advice of the first caring adult you talk to, it is better not to leap to a decision.

31 How can I get an abortion without my parents finding out?

The rules governing parental knowledge or consent are constantly changing. It depends upon the state in which you live and the rules of the specific clinic. Some states and some clinics require parental **permission** if the woman is under eighteen years of age, others require merely notification of the parents, some do not require any contact with the parents at all. It is best to check with your local family planning clinic for this information.

32 How can I be sure I am capable of having children?

Most men and women are capable of becoming fathers and mothers. If you are a normal healthy teenager from a family with no serious, hereditary health problems and so is your partner, you can be ninety-nine percent certain that you can have children. Instead of worrying about it, it makes more sense to put your energy into keeping healthy by eating properly and exercising regularly, by having all diseases, including venereal diseases, treated promptly and by avoiding both illegal drugs and excessive use of prescription and over-the-counter medicines.

33 If you become pregnant after you have had intercourse with several boys, can you tell who the father is?

Once the baby is born, you can. There are tests that can determine who the father is by comparing his genetic material to that of the baby.

34 Can you get pregnant during your menstrual period?

Although the egg is usually no longer able to be fertilized, and is expelled during menstruation, it is still possible for a woman to get pregnant at this time. It is especially likely for a teenage girl, because her cycles may be irregular for the first year or so, and an egg may be ripe when she doesn't expect it. She may also mistake the irregular discharges of blood called "spotting" for her period. It is better not to have intercourse, or to use reliable birth control methods.

35 Why do women die in childbirth?

This happens now very rarely. In the past, people didn't realize how important it was for a woman to have a clean, germ free environment in which to give birth, and so many women contracted life-threatening infections. Today it usually happens because the woman already had some serious health problem, and the extra strain of giving birth was too much for her body to stand.

However, even a woman with a health problem now stands little chance of dying in child birth, provided she visits her doctor regularly before she gives birth. The doctor can detect any health problem and keep it under control. But what often happens instead is that the woman only seeks medical help when she is about to give birth. Then it is too late to find or treat other medical problems. Instead her health problem is made worse by the strain of giving birth, and can end up killing her or her baby.

36 Can you tell the sex of a baby before it is born?

Yes you can. There is a test, called **amniocentesis**, that can be given to a mother while she is pregnant to see if the baby is developing normally. The main reason for giving it is not to find out the baby's sex, but to make sure the baby is not retarded or seriously defective in some other way. From this test doctors can tell whether the baby is a boy or girl.

Amniocentesis has some risks, and is also quite expensive. Most people do not choose to have this test just to find out the baby's sex. Even parents who do have the test done often ask the doctor not to tell them. Most parents are happy regardless of whether they have a girl or a boy.

37 Can a girl have a baby without a father?

No. A girl or woman can certainly have a baby without a husband, but some boy or man must be the father. Even a baby that starts life in a laboratory dish must have a father.

38 Can a baby have more than one father?

A baby can only have one natural father. Only one sperm cell among the many millions that can be inside a woman will enter an ovum (egg) to begin a new life, and this sperm can only have come from one man. A woman could have sex with more than one man close together, so it would be hard to know who the father is if she became pregnant. But the lone sperm that fertilized the ovum that grew into that particular baby can only have come from one man. Now, with recently developed genetic tests, a laboratory would be able to tell who is the father, if there were any doubt.

A baby may also have an adoptive father. If the natural father is unable or unwilling to take care of the baby, or perhaps dies, then another man can become the legal father of the baby by going to court. The adoptive father has freely chosen to become father of the child, and almost always loves the child as much as if it grew from his own sperm.

39 How do twins happen?

There are two ways. First, when a single fertilized egg, fertilized by a single sperm, divides into two new cells, each cell starts growing into a different child. In this case, the twins will be identical twins or one egg twins.

Second, occasionally the woman produces two ova (eggs) at the same time, instead of just one. Both eggs may become fertilized by two different sperm at about the same time, and grow into two babies. These are called fraternal or two-egg twins; they are not identical. It is also possible to have three babies (triplets), four babies (quadruplets) and even five babies (quintuplets) at the same time. In fact, the most babies ever born at the same time is nine.

Identical twins are almost exactly alike because they share the same genetic material, the set of instructions that tells the body how to grow. Fraternal twins, beginning as separate sperm-egg combinations, each have different genetic material, do not look alike and may be different genders.

When twins are born, they come down the birth canal (vagina) one at a time—sometimes only a few minutes apart, sometimes a half hour or more apart.

40 What are Siamese twins?

Siamese twins are twins who are attached to each other. They may share only some skin or flesh, or they may share internal organs.

41 How can Siamese twins be separated?

If they are only connected by skin or some unimportant piece of flesh, the separation is relatively easy. If they share internal organs, it is much more difficult. If they are not separated, they usually do not live more than five years and they cannot live normal lives, so doctors always decide to separate them. If they are both sharing a vital organ, one may have to die so that the other one can live. This is a terrible choice for a parent to have to make. Fortunately, it is extremely rare.

42 How long does a baby remain inside the mother? Can it live if it is born before the normal time has passed?

Usually, a baby takes about forty weeks—or nine months—from the time it is conceived until it is ready to be born. At that time, it has developed enough to be able to live on its own. Some babies stay inside the womb for ten months.

Sometimes a baby is born early, after only seven or eight months. This is called a **premature baby.** There is nothing wrong with being born early or late.

Most babies born after seven months can now survive, but they usually require special hospital care to help them until they develop more. In recent years, scientists and doctors have greatly improved the chances for young babies who would have surely died only a few years ago.

However, the baby is better off staying inside its mother's womb for the full nine months. Early and regular medical attention make this far more likely to happen.

43 What is a miscarriage?

A miscarriage is the expulsion of a fetus from the womb long before it can survive by itself. The fetus leaves the uterus through the birth canal or vagina. It comes out as part of a bloody discharge.

A miscarriage can be emotionally very painful for the expectant mother and father, because they may have already imagined the fetus as a baby, and have great hopes and plans for it. Actually the fetus is usually still very tiny, not even recognizable as a human baby. Often it is expelled because there is something wrong and the fetus cannot grow into a normal, healthy person. The woman's body has the amazing ability to check the fetus and see whether it is growing properly. If it finds something seriously wrong, it can cause the fetus to be expelled. It is nature's way of eliminating a defective fetus that could not have survived even if it had remained inside for the full nine months. We don't always know why a miscarriage has happened or understand very well how the body decides to expel a fetus.

A miscarriage does not mean that there is something wrong with the mother. One in six pregnancies ends in miscarriage, but it is quite likely that the next pregnancy will be a normal one.

44 Is a baby inside of a sack when it is inside its mother?

Yes. Not only is it inside the uterus, which is a muscle, but it also floats inside a sack called the "amniotic sack," which is like a bag filled with fluid. This sack and fluid help protect the baby while it is inside the mother. This bag of fluid breaks just before the baby is born, so that the baby can get out. After the baby is born, the bag comes out too, and is discarded.

45 How does the baby eat and drink and breathe before it is born? How can it live inside the mother?

The baby is fed through a tube called the umbilical cord connecting it to its mother. It is attached at the baby's belly button or navel. In this way, it takes in food and water from the mother's bloodstream. We also know that it may drink some of the amniotic fluid, but we don't know why.

The baby also receives the oxygen from her blood that it will later get from the air by breathing. For this reason, it does not need to breathe while inside the mother, and can float comfortably, completely surrounded by the amniotic fluid without drowning or starving.

46 Where does the fetus's waste go?

All of it is carried from the baby's blood through the umbilical cord into the mother's bloodstream, where it is filtered out by the mother's kidneys.

47 What are the stages of pre-natal development? What does the baby do while it is inside its mother?

At first, not much. Very early in its development, its heart begins to beat. Later, it begins to move its arms and legs. As it grows bigger, the pregnant woman can feel the baby's movements, and she and the father can even see and feel them on the mother's belly. Babies can even suck their thumbs inside the uterus, and scientists believe that they can hear noises from outside. They also sleep a great deal.

It takes about ten days for fertilization and implantation (attachment of the fetus to the uterine lining) to be completed. At the end of four weeks, the fetus is approximately a quarter of an inch long. Its heart is pumping blood. At the end of eight weeks, it is about three-quarters of an inch long. Its limbs are beginning to develop and the umbilical cord has formed. By the end of twelve weeks, it has grown to nearly three inches long, weighs about one ounce and its arms, hands, fingers and legs have formed. The fetus has eyes and its heartbeat can be detected by the doctor.

During the fourth month of pregnancy, the fetus has grown to seven inches long, weighs about four ounces and has a strong digestive system.

In the fifth month, the baby's lungs have developed so that it could survive if born at this time.

By the sixth month, the baby is about eleven to fourteen inches long, weighs about one and one-half pounds, is quite wrinkled and is covered with a heavy protective creamy coating. The fingernails have developed at this point.

At the seventh month, the baby's weight doubles in the last three months. By the eighth month, the last two months of growth are very important to the baby. The baby is about eighteen inches long. In the ninth month, the baby's average weight is about seven pounds and its length is around twenty inches. By this time, the baby's development is completed and the birthing process begins.[4]

48 When the baby kicks inside the mother, does it injure her?

Kicking does not damage the mother, because the baby is inside the amniotic sack, which contains much fluid. For this reason, it cannot directly kick any part of the mother's body, and cannot hurt the mother, although it may be somewhat uncomfortable for the mother.

More often the baby's kicking is exciting, because it is the first sign that the baby is an active and aware person. In the Bible the first time the mother feels the baby moved is called "quickening," and some theologians (religious thinkers) believed that it was at this point that the soul entered the fetus.

49 Is sexual intercourse OK during pregnancy?

Having sex during pregnancy does not usually hurt the mother or the baby. A new baby cannot get started once one is already developing inside her. During intercourse, the man places his penis in the woman's vagina. The baby is not in the vagina, but in the uterus, located above it. Moreover, it is further enclosed in a sealed sack of fluid, the amniotic sack.

The main danger is that if the man has a venereal disease and gives it to the woman. Venereal disease (VD) can harm both the fetus and the mother. If you don't know whether your partner has such a disease, you are running the risk of hurting yourself and your baby.

There are some conditions in which it is considered better for the woman not to have intercourse during pregnancy. Your doctor will tell you if this is the case. Also, it may be uncomfortable for the woman to have intercourse lying on her back, so you may want to try other positions. Late in pregnancy, sexual activity may be too uncomfortable for the woman to enjoy it.

50 If a pregnant woman falls, will it hurt the baby?

Usually it will not. Of course, if a pregnant woman falls off a mountain both she and the baby will be very badly hurt! But in more usual falls, the fetus has several layers of protection. It is located inside the uterus, which has very strong muscular walls. Also, the baby is inside another sack—the amniotic sack—where it floats in a fluid. It is about as difficult to hurt a baby inside its mother as it is to hurt someone in a swimming pool by punching the water!

51 Why do pregnant women sometimes crave certain foods?

We don't always know. Sometimes, the woman may just want to give herself a special treat like ice cream.

52 Is it true that a pregnant woman must "eat for two?"

No, this is a myth. If the mother puts on a lot of weight, most of it will be fat that she will probably want to lose after the baby is born. Gaining excess weight will put a strain on the mother's body. A woman should not gain more than about 25 pounds during pregnancy. It is also not the time to go on a weight-reduction diet, because both the baby and the mother need certain nutrients and minerals.

However, it is **very** important that she eat nourishing foods—hot dogs, french fries and milk shakes are not the way to nourish a growing baby or its mother! The baby does not need large quantities of food, but it needs the whole range of nutrients to grow properly. It is important that the mother eat a balanced diet of meat, fish, fruits, vegetables and cereals. Fiber-rich foods like dark-grain breads, fruits and some cereals may also prevent constipation, a frequent annoyance during pregnancy.

53 Do babies born to teen mothers die more often and have more birth defects than others? What is the biggest cause of birth defects?

Age is the single greatest cause of birth defects—the mother is either too old or too young. Unfortunately most babies with birth defects are born to teenage mothers, and more such babies die soon after birth. (For older mothers see Question 12, above.) Most occurrences of sudden infant death syndrome (or "crib death") happen to them. (See CRIB DEATHS in the Glossary.) A teenage girl's body is still growing while it is also trying to nourish a growing baby. Her body may not have an adequate supply of proteins, vitamins and minerals for both mother and child, and the baby can lose out. Of course not every child of a teenage mother will have problems, and in fact the mother can prevent most harm by taking the right steps.

The most important step is to go to a doctor right away if you even suspect that you are pregnant. The first three months are the time of most rapid development for the fetus, and it is then that any lack of nourishment or other harmful condition in the mother can do the most serious damage. A doctor will help you make sure you eat the right foods to have a healthy baby, and correct any problems right away.

54 Why are some babies born deformed? Is smoking harmful? What about drinking and drugs?

We do not know all the causes of deformities, but we do know some that the mother can easily avoid. If the mother smokes a great deal, the baby can be born weighing about a half pound less than it would normally. If the baby is already very small for other reasons, the half-pound may mean the difference between life and death. The baby can also have nicotine—one of the major harmful ingredients in cigarette smoke—in its blood. This substance can disrupt the baby's development. Nicotine is also what makes cigarette smoking addictive. The baby too may become addicted to nicotine, and will have to go through nicotine withdrawal—a very painful experience, and one that is especially terrifying for a new-born who has no idea what is happening.

Alcohol is also very harmful. It passes from the mother's blood through the umbilical cord into the baby's blood, where it can get to the baby's brain. Especially in the earlier stages of pregnancy, when the brain and other organs are still forming, the alcohol may damage and deform them. Doctors strongly recommend that pregnant women do not drink alcohol.

Cocaine, and especially "crack," are very dangerous for the fetus. Often they cause the baby to be born too soon, and with an addiction to the drug. The arms and legs of such babies often shake uncontrollably, and they are likely to have breathing and other problems. There are few things more tragic than a tiny, drug-addicted infant.

Heroine, "speed," "uppers," "downers" and LSD may all seriously harm a developing fetus. We are not sure about the effects of marijuana, but it is best to be safe and avoid it during pregnancy. Even prescription or non-prescription drugs like aspirin that are fine at other times may harm the fetus. A pregnant women should take **no** drugs unless her doctor gives the OK. Anything you eat or drink is likely to get to the vulnerable fetus, so a good rule is to never take any medication without checking it out with your doctor or nurse-practitioner.

55 Can venereal disease harm the fetus?

Yes it can. It is very important for every pregnant woman to have a VD test. Usually, the disease can be treated so that it does not harm the baby.

Syphilis can infect the baby and cause it to be born with a defect. Gonorrhea can infect the baby as it comes down the birth canal. This kind of venereal disease can blind, or even kill, the baby.

AIDS, or acquired immune deficiency syndrome, may be passed from the mother to the fetus and cause the baby to die.

56 Can the parents tell if they are going to have a deformed baby?

They can't by themselves, but doctors now detect many disorders that cause children to have birth defects. The most well-known test is

amniocentesis. This is usually performed on mothers in their thirties or older, or if the doctor suspects a defect.

There are also tests that can be performed on the parents to determine whether they are carriers of genetic diseases. Different racial and ethnic groups are known to carry particular genetic disorders. If they are found to be carriers, then amniocentesis often shows whether they have transmitted the disorder to a specific fetus early in pregnancy.

There are a number of reasons for birth defects. One may be genetic— this means that something is wrong with one of the inherited genes from the mother or father or both. Mutations may cause birth defects. This means that a gene has changed and the change causes a defect. Sometimes the baby has an extra chromosome. Usually, the baby has forty-six chromosomes, but a baby with a birth defect may have forty-seven.

Problems in the baby's environment may cause a defect. For example, the mother may not have been able to obtain the proper nutrition, she had an infection that affected the baby or she drank, smoked or took drugs or medicines that damaged the baby. Although we know very little about it, there can also be effects of the larger environment, such as radiation or pollution.

The March of Dimes organization works hard to raise money to understand and treat many different birth defects. They list the following birth defects as the most common inherited defects: sickle cell anemia affects one in ten African-Americans; thalassemia mostly affects persons of Italian or Greek descent; Try-Sachs affects babies of Jewish descent; PKU affects mostly persons of northern European descent; the Rh disease affects the blood (there is now a vaccine for this); spina bifida affects the infant's spine; Downs syndrome, including mental retardation, is caused by the presence of an extra chromosome; marfan syndrome is an abnormality of the bones and ligiments; achrondrophasia brings about a shortening of the arms and legs; and neurofibromatosis causes spots on the baby's skin.

57 What happens if a girl who is not in good health becomes pregnant?

It all depends upon what problem she has. Kidney or bladder diseases can be made worse by pregnancy, and also put the fetus in danger. It is best for a woman to have a complete physical examination before she becomes pregnant so that any health problems can be identified and treated first. If a woman has an on-going, chronic illness, she should discuss it with her doctor before she decides to get pregnant.

It is especially important that a woman with a health problem who does become pregnant see her doctor immediately.

58 Why can't some people have children? Why do some people adopt children?

There are many reasons. A man can have no sperm or too few sperm to make a woman pregnant. A woman may have some problem with her fallopian tubes or her uterus. In the last few years scientists have developed ways of treating and curing many of these problems. For example, if a woman's tubes are blocked, an egg may be extracted from her ovary, and sperm-containing semen taken from her husband. Then both the egg and sperm are placed in a glass laboratory dish, where the sperm cell fertilizes the egg. This is called **in-vitro** fertilization (from the Latin for "in the glass"). The fertilized egg is then placed in the uterus. If the man has no sperm, sperm from another man, called a donor, may be inserted into the woman's uterus so that she can become pregnant.

If nothing works, the couple may often adopt a child. Tragically, there are many children whose parents are unable and unwilling to take care of them, and need new parents. Parents find that they love an adopted child just as much as if they were of the same flesh and blood.

B. CHILDBIRTH

59 What is being born?

Both humans and animals start out in the world by being born. Some animals are born from an egg, while others come live directly out of their mothers. Human beings come directly out of their mothers' bodies, where they have been growing for nine months. After this amount of time, they are strong enough to breathe for themselves, eat food through their mouths, and to continue to develop separately from the mother's body.

60 How can the mother tell when the baby is ready to be born?

First of all, shortly before birth, the bag of waters or amniotic sack, which holds the baby, breaks and the fluid comes out through the woman's vagina. Second, the mother feels the contractions of the uterus as they begin to push the baby down and out of her body. At first, the contractions come far apart and are relatively small. As the time of birth approaches, the contractions come more and more often, becoming stronger and stronger.

61 How does birth take place? What makes the baby come out?

Before birth, the mother's uterus begins a long series of contractions. This is called labor. Labor may begin as small back pains or cramps. These warn the mother that she will soon give birth. They gradually become closer together and more powerful. As the contractions continue, they push the baby down against the cervix or neck of the uterus, causing it to expand or dilate. When the contractions are three to five minutes apart, the mother is ready to go to the hospital or other place where she will give birth.

When the cervix is fully dilated and open, the contractions press the baby down into the vagina. The baby's head is the widest part of its body, and is about four inches (10 centimeters) wide. The vagina, usually a fairly narrow tube, has the truly amazing ability to stretch and expand, enabling the baby's body to pass through it. Although it is pushed with considerable force by the uterus, the baby is not injured.

At birth, the baby is still connected to the mother by a cord called the umbilical cord. This tube supplied nourishment and oxygen to the baby while it was inside the mother, and served to remove waste from it. Now the baby no longer needs it, so someone—usually the doctor or nurse-practitioner—ties it off and cuts it. This is painless for both mother and child.

The baby will probably be placed on the mother's body for a few seconds to let it know who its mother is. This is called bonding, and is believed to strengthen the baby's sense of security by letting it feel its mother's touch. After a brief check that it is breathing and responding normally (called the Apgar test), the baby is handed to the mother and father to hold, so that bonding may continue. This gives it its first experience of belonging to a family with this particular mother and father, and no other.

After awhile, the baby may be taken away to the nursery to be watched for a few hours. You should find out what your doctor and your hospital usually do. You may not wish to be separated from your baby for such a long time, and should make this clear to both doctor and hospital beforehand. Many hospitals have birthing suites that are more like a home bedroom, in which the parents and baby can stay together.

With a few more contractions, the after-birth is expelled. This consists of the placenta, the organ which attached the cord to the mother, and the amniotic sack in which the baby was sheltered. Shortly after birth, the vagina returns to its normal size, and the uterus shrinks back to its usual size (about the size of the woman's fist). The mother often goes home within twenty-four to forty-eight hours after she has given birth, but she will need help with the newborn baby when she gets home. Although the baby can now live outside the mother's body, it will still need years of care before it lives apart from its parents.

Have you ever seen a new born baby? It is very small and helpless, and is usually either hungry or tired. It can't yet see much more than a foot or so in front of its face, it can't crawl or control its fingers, hands, arms and legs very well. But in a few short months it will be grasping things, playing with its hands and feet, following objects with its eyes, smiling and giggling. Within about a year it may be crawling, walking and trying to talk!

62 How do twins and triplets come out at birth?

They come out one at a time—thank goodness! There are a few minutes or even an hour or so between the births. That's why it is often said that one twin is the older of the two. It is even possible for twins not to have the same birthday, if one is born just before midnight and the other just after.

63 What else comes out of the mother besides the baby?

Shortly before birth, the amniotic sack or "bag of waters" in which the baby is floating breaks. The amniotic fluid, which is watery, flows out of the vagina. After the child is born, the placenta or "afterbirth" also comes out. This organ connected the umbilical cord to the mother. It is no longer needed and is disgarded.

64 Does it hurt to have a baby?

Giving birth is the hardest work a woman ever does, and there is considerable pain involved. How much can vary from woman to woman and from baby to baby. The contractions of the uterus can be quite painful for the mother. They are like strong cramps. Fortunately the contractions are not constant, but come and go. In between the contractions, the mother has a chance to rest. Labor can last as little as one hour, and as long as ten to twelve hours. Sometimes a woman who has already had a child will have a shorter labor with her next child.

However if you see a film of a woman giving birth, you may get the impression that there is more pain involved than there really is. The mother often strains hard to push the baby out, and this can look like she is crying in pain.

As the baby is being pushed out, the woman's body is wonderfully set up so that it becomes deadened to some of the pain. Most mothers feel that having a wonderful new child is worth the pain, and quickly forget it once they are holding their new born child in their arms.

65 Can the mother do anything to make the birth less painful? Can the father help too?

Yes, there are some things that both the mother- and father-to-be can do to reduce the discomfort of labor and childbirth. They can learn breathing exercises that help relax the mother and make the birth process easier. The mother can learn to help the contractions along by pushing at the right moment. She can also learn to relax the muscles in the lower part of her body. Often, the mother- and father-to-be take classes that teach them these and other techniques, and what to expect. Many hospitals offer such classes. The doctor may give some medication to the mother during the birth process to help ease the severity of the contractions. Many fathers have told me that seeing their child's birth and helping and supporting the mother through her labor was one of the most exciting events of their lives.[5]

66 If you don't go to the hospital to deliver the baby, will you die?

There is a somewhat greater chance that the mother or child will have problems if they do not have the help of a doctor and a hospital. But it is very rare now for a mother to die during childbirth. If the mother does not go to the hospital, the labor process will continue, the uterus will dilate and the baby will be born anyway. Mothers do need someone to assist them in the birthing process.

67 Why does my mother have to go to the hospital to have a baby?

A pregnant woman does not have to go to the hospital to have her baby. Until the twentieth century, most babies were born at home. But now we think it is usually safer for both the baby and the mother to have the baby in the hospital. The hospital has special rooms set up just for having babies. They are called labor rooms and delivery rooms. There are doctors and nurses who are specifically trained to help women give birth, and have assisted at many births. Occasionally, the mother or baby may have some difficulties during the birth process. The hospital also has all the assistance and equipment that the doctors and nurses might need to help the mother give birth if there is some problem.

68 If the baby is born in a hospital, can the baby's father be present at the birth?

In most cases he certainly can. You can inquire about this before the baby is born. Most couples prefer that the father be present. The father can help the mother by comforting her, reminding her of the proper way to breathe that they have learned to reduce the pain and discomfort and by massaging her. Both he and the mother will be able to hold the baby shortly after it is born.

69 What does the doctor do?

The mother does most of the work. The mother and father usually like having the doctor present so that they are reassured that everything is going OK. The doctor makes sure that labor is proceeding the way it should. He or she may advise the mother on how to help the process along by pushing at certain times, and not pushing at others. The doctor may help reduce some of the pain, although now many women and many doctors feel that pain killers during labor are not a very good idea, because these medicines can have a bad effect on the baby, and also make it harder for the mother to actively help the process along.

As the baby is being born, the doctor helps it come out smoothly. Then he or she cuts the cord, and delivers the afterbirth. Finally, the doctor cleans off the baby and makes sure that it is breathing properly, and helps the mother begin her recovery from labor.

70 Can the baby be hurt if it is pulled out?

The doctor doesn't pull the baby out; he or she waits for the mother to push it out naturally. When the baby's head is almost fully out, the doctor will hold it up, because the baby cannot yet hold up its own head and its neck might be injured if its head flopped down suddenly.

Sometimes the baby may become somewhat stuck, and the doctor may use a special instrument called forceps to help the baby come out. This instrument enables the doctor to gently guide the baby's head in such a way that it is not injured.

71 Does the baby always come out head first? What causes a "breech" delivery?

The baby usually comes out head first, but it is not the only way. They can come out feet first or buttocks first. This is called a breech birth. It can be more painful for the mother, because the head is the biggest part of the baby's body, and if the feet or buttocks come out first, the cervix may still have to expand further to allow the head out. This may add some time to the labor. (Normally, once the head is out the rest of the body slips out easily.) Sometimes the doctor can detect ahead of time that the baby is not in the correct position, and help it turn the right way before birth.

Even when head first, the baby can come out facing the wrong way. Usually it is facing downward, toward its mother's back, but sometimes it is facing upward, toward her stomach. None of these positions hurts the baby in any way.

The baby usually comes out head first because the head is the heaviest and largest part of the body, and so is usually at the lowest point Much of the time, the baby grows in this position. The baby is not uncomfortable being upside down because it is floating in the amniotic fluid and has no sense of direction.

72 How do they cut the umbilical cord? Does it hurt the baby or the mother?

The cord is cut about an inch or so from the baby's navel (belly button). It is tied on either side of the place where the cut will be made to prevent excess bleeding. The cord has no pain nerves in it, so neither the mother nor the baby feels any pain.

In ten days to two weeks, the navel heals and the small remaining piece of the umbilical cord dries up and falls off. A bandage may be placed over the navel until it heals.

73 What happens if the umbilical cord gets wrapped around the baby's neck?

The umbilical cord is about three feet long, and about the thickness of your thumb. If it does get wrapped around the baby's neck inside the mother, it doesn't injure the baby. This is because the baby is not breathing through its nose, mouth and throat, but is absorbing oxygen through the cord. If the cord becomes wrapped around the baby's neck, sooner or later it will get unwrapped as the baby moves around.

During birth, however, there is some danger that the cord will get pinched during the birth process and cut off the baby's oxygen, or be wrapped around the baby's neck at birth. That is why most women prefer to have their babies in a hospital or medically staffed birthing facility, so that doctors with appropriate equipment and knowledge are available if something like this happens. But such complications are not very common.

74 Does a woman have to be sewn up after the birth?

Most of the time the vagina will expand enough to allow the baby to come out. Sometimes, the doctor may fear that the baby's birth will tear the delicate tissue of the vagina, and so makes a small incision (cut). This is called an episiotomy. After the birth, it will be sewn up with a few stitches, usually with a local anaesthetic. The cut heals in a few days.

75 Does the doctor slap the baby on the rear after it is born?

No. This is how it is often shown on television. In real life, the doctor may rub the baby on its back to make it cry and begin breathing, but often the baby starts crying all by itself. When it cries, it fills its lungs with air and starts to breath on its own. The baby's cry is reassuring to parents and doctor, because it shows that the baby is breathing properly.

76 What does it feel like to be born?

We don't really know. No one can remember what it was like. Perhaps it is a bit of a shock. Until you were born, all that you had ever known was the experience of floating calmly in your mother's womb. Suddenly, you feel the walls of the uterus pressing against you, and you are pushed down into a narrow space, the vagina. Even though it is wide enough to let you through, it is only *just* wide enough. And of course you can't ask your parents or anyone else what's happening!

Perhaps this is why many babies cry right after they are born. But the experience doesn't seem to hurt the baby; as soon as it is held and nursed, it stops crying. Often, the baby goes to sleep right after it is born. It has been hard work for the baby, just as it has been for the mother. Babies usually sleep a great deal for the first few weeks after they are born.

77 Why do some mothers have their babies by an operation on their bellies? What is a caesarean delivery?

A caesarean delivery is delivery of the baby by surgically removing it from the mother. The Roman ruler and general Julius Caesar was delivered in this way.

Occasionally, there is a problem during labor and delivery, and the doctor feels that the baby is not coming out fast enough. Sometimes the mother is in labor for a long time, but her cervix does not dilate. Sometimes the bag of waters (amniotic sack) breaks, but labor does not start. Then a caesarean delivery or "C-section" is performed.

In a caesarean delivery, a surgical incision (cut) is made in the mother's lower belly, the uterus is opened, and the baby is removed. Then her uterus and her belly are sewn up. The operation is done with an anaesthetic, so the mother does not experience pain. This operation can be done painlessly without putting the mother to sleep, so she can see and hold her new baby right after it is born. The father can also be present—a screen is put up across the mother's belly to maintain a sterile operating field.

The mother may have to stay in the hospital a little longer than after a vaginal birth—about one week.

78 Are caesarean births safe?

A caesarean delivery is not a very dangerous operation, but like all surgical operations, it is a serious one and carries some risks. Many people believe that too many caesarean deliveries are being performed. It should never be done just for the convenience of the mother or the doctor. Unless there is some problem in the normal birth process, it is safer for both mother and baby for the birth to proceed in the normal way. The normal birth process seems to set the baby's body working properly.

The overwhelming majority of babies born either way are healthy and normal, but a caesarean delivery should not be undertaken unless there is a clear reason for it. While many doctors believe that a woman who has had one caesarean delivery should always be delivered in this way, in recent years this attitude has been changing. This is something you need to discuss with your doctor ahead of time.

79 What is an incubator?

This is a special compartment with a bed in which a baby may be placed. It is used mostly for premature babies (babies born early). It provides warmth and perhaps breathing assistance for the baby until it has grown and developed enough to live normally. Usually, the baby is placed in a special hospital unit where it can be watched and its breathing and heartbeat can be observed constantly. The baby may remain in an incubator from a few days to a few weeks. Usually the earlier the baby is born, the longer it will have to stay in the incubator.

Sometimes, a full-term baby with breathing problems may also be placed in one. Any baby born weighing less than four-and one-half pounds will be given care in a special nursery, and may be put in an incubator.

80 What is a "blue baby"?

A "blue baby" is one that is born with a problem with its blood circulation. The blood carries the oxygen to all the cells of the body. If not enough blood and oxygen are getting to a part of the body, it will appear blue. You can see this if you pinch your finger. First it will turn red, then blue as the oxygen in the blood trapped in your finger is used up. This is what is happening all over the body of a "blue baby."

Often doctors can operate to correct the problem, which is often a problem in the heart, such as a hole in a wall, or a valve that does not close properly. Once the problem is corrected, such babies can usually go on to lead normal lives.

81 How much does a newborn baby weigh?

A baby can weigh anywhere from five to eleven or more pounds. A premature baby (a baby born before full term) may weigh only a little more than a pound. When a baby is born with a low birth rate there is reason for concern, but it is likely that the baby will grow normally. A baby may lose an ounce or two right after birth, but resumes putting on weight very rapidly for the first few months.

82 How does the newborn baby eat?

The baby eats by sucking milk from a nipple. The nipple can either be on the mother's breast, or on a bottle with specially prepared milk (formula). A baby has a very strong urge to suck, and often wants to suck even when it is not hungry.

It is usually best to breastfeed the baby. Nursing at the breast is much more comforting to the baby than drinking from a bottle. Babies almost always look very happy and content while nursing at their mother's breast. Nevertheless, all that sucking is hard work, and often tires the baby out so that it falls asleep.

The mother's milk is also just right for the baby's nourishment. It contains special chemicals called **antibodies** that protect the baby from many kinds of infectious diseases. Also, many young babies are allergic to cow's milk. (However, there are formulas that do not contain cow's milk, but use other ingredients like soy milk.) Newborn babies cannot eat solid food.

Mothers who work outside the home can even store breast milk for their baby by using a breast pump. That way, their breasts do not become uncomfortably full during the day when they are away from their babies, and the baby has breast milk even when the mother is not available.

83 How does milk get into the breasts? Can you get milk only when you have a baby?

During pregnancy, the woman's breasts become larger, as thousands of tiny glands inside them grow larger in preparation for producing milk.

Right at birth the breasts contain colostrum, which contains proteins and antibodies and is quite nourishing for the baby. The baby begins nursing on this fluid right away, until the breasts begin to produce milk. When the baby leaves its mother's body, the change sends a chemical message to the breasts to produce milk. The baby's sucking also powerfully stimulates the breasts to produce milk. Once the breasts have begun producing milk, they adjust how much they make to how much the baby drinks. The mother needs to feed the baby at least once every 24 hours and to suckle the baby at both breasts, to keep the breasts producing milk. If they are not stimulated for much longer than a day, they will stop producing. Of course, a baby should be fed much more often than once per day, even if it is not breastfed.

Once the baby stops nursing, the breasts will stop producing milk. Only if a woman has another child will they again produce milk in large quantities. If a woman decides not to nurse, the doctor can give her medication that will quickly stop milk production.[6]

84 How long after a woman gives birth does she begin to menstruate again?

This varies, but usually about six weeks or so after she gives birth she will resume her menstrual cycle. But even before this time, she can become pregnant again.

REFERENCES

1. Guttmacher, Alan. *Teenage Pregnancy: The Problem That Hasn't Gone Away.* New York: Alan Guttmacher Institute, 1981, pp. 28–36.
2. Bell, R. *Changing Bodies, Changing Lives.* New York: Random House, 1980, p. 190.
3. Ibid. (Guttmacher) pp. 16–21.
4. Calderone, M. and Johnson, E. *Family Book of Sexuality.* New York: Bantam Books, 1983, pp. 62–75.
5. Boston Women's Health Book Collective. *Our Bodies Ourselves.* New York: Simon and Schuster, 1976, pp. 274–283.
6. Ibid (Calderone) pp. 76–78.

Chapter III

RELATIONSHIPS

A. PARENT, CHILD AND FAMILY

1 Can you send a baby back?

No, you cannot. A baby, like any other child, needs someone to take care of him or her. Babies need more care than older children. When you were first born, your parents spent a lot of time feeding you, playing with you, changing your diapers and keeping you clean and healthy. Now that you are more grown up, you can take care of yourself with less help from your parents. If you have a baby brother or sister, your parents probably spend more time with him or her than with you. This does not mean they love you less than the baby. It simply means that the baby needs more care than you do—she cannot crawl, walk, talk, go to the bathroom by herself, say what she needs or find her own toys.

2 Why are some children adopted?

Sometimes a man is not capable of fathering a child, or a woman is not capable of becoming pregnant. Perhaps the man doesn't produce enough sperm or the woman has some problem with ripening eggs, or getting them from her ovaries to her uterus. In the last few years, scientists and doctors have discovered many new ways of helping people with medical problems like these, but sometimes a couple simply can't have children. When a couple cannot have children of their own, they often adopt one.

All children need parents to take care of them, give them a home and make them feel safe and happy. The adopted child did have a mother and father when he or she was born, but the parents did not have a home where they could take care of the baby. The new parents do have a home, and they love their child just as much as if he or she had been born to them. Parents love a child mainly because they live with and take care of him or her. Even when a child is not adopted and lives with its natural parents, the parents and child's loving feelings continue to develop as the child grows. You can't tell by looking at someone or by how he or she acts if he or she is adopted or not. If a child is not getting along with his or her parents, this usually has little to do with whether or not the child is adopted.

3 Do you have to be married to have a baby?

No. A girl or woman may become pregnant and have a baby any-time after she is about twelve years old. Usually, a girl does not want to get pregnant and have a baby that early. She wants to grow up and have all of the fun of being grown up for awhile. It's very hard to work full-time, go to school or even go to a movie for the parent of a young child.

It takes a lot of time and money to take care of a baby. Babies are better off with both a father and a mother to take care of them, so it's best for a girl to be married before she has a baby.

4 Why do Daddy and Mommy close the door when they go to sleep?

Everyone likes to have a private time and a private place. At home, when the bedroom door is closed, it usually means that the people inside want to have their private time. They may just want to talk without being interrupted. Or, they may want to make love, and people almost always prefer to make love in private. It is a good idea to knock on the door when it is closed and wait for your parents to tell you that it's OK to come in.

We all like to have a private place. Even though you love your parents very much, you probably don't want to be with them all the time. You probably already have things that you feel are private and that you do not want to share with anyone else. It is nice to know you can go into your room or someplace else for a short while and not have anyone bother you. If you do not have a place in your house where you can be alone, you can ask about this.

5 Why can't I marry Daddy (Mommy)?

Mothers and fathers can only be married to one person at a time. Your mommy and daddy are already married to each other. But each of us can love more than one person at a time. Your mommy and daddy love you very much, but they love you differently than they love each other. They love you as a son or daughter. If you are a girl, some day you will grow up and meet a nice man just as your mommy met your daddy, and you may decide to marry that man. If you are a boy, when you get big you will meet a nice woman just as your daddy met your mommy, and perhaps marry her.

6 Can I watch mommy and daddy have sex?

No. This is something private between your mother and father.

7 Why do some couples not have children?

A man and woman can decide when to have children. Although they may be having sex, including sexual intercourse, they may use birth control methods of various kinds to avoid having a child. Why do they decide not to have one? Often they are waiting until they have finished school, found steady jobs they like and saved up some money. Perhaps they want to buy a house first.

Taking care of a new baby is a lot of extra work for both parents. The parents may have to get up several times each night for a long time. A new baby is something that it is best to be well prepared for!

8 Why doesn't my friend next door have a father?

It is possible that he has died, but it is much more likely that your friend's parents are divorced. For some reason they disagreed so much about so many things that they decided to separate, and are no longer married. Sometimes the mother takes care of the children, sometimes both parents do and sometimes the father alone takes care of them. Usually both parents contribute to the support of the child.

It is not the child's fault that his parents have been divorced. Both the mother and father love the child just as much as they did before. It is always very hard on everyone in the family when parents separate or get a divorce. Most parents do not do so until they have thought long and hard about it, and have decided they are too unhappy living with each other to continue.

9 How do you make your mom and dad stop treating you like a baby?

There is no easy answer. Parents often worry about their children's safety and well being. They have read and heard about so much that can happen to children and teenagers; teen drinking, drug use and pregnancy are in the news every day. They want to be sure that you can take care of yourself before they give you more freedom. Try to imagine yourself in their position. Imagine that you have a child whom you love very much and worry about all the time. Do you think that you would be eager to see that child stay out late by himself or herself with other young people you don't know very well?

You can begin by asking your parents what you can do to be treated in a more grown up way. You can ask for new privileges, but only one at a time. Try to talk to them calmly; getting into an argument or a shouting match will not convince them that you are more grown up—even if they lose their temper first. If they say something that hurts your feelings, try not to get angry. Instead, calmly let them know that they said something that hurt you. If you do this, they will be amazed at how grown up you have become!

You can also begin on your own to act more grown up. You can try to be more responsible—do your share of the dishes or clean your room without being reminded. You can help out when you aren't asked to. You can try to be more dependable by arriving home when you say you will, or calling them if you can't make it. If they learn they can depend on and trust you, they may begin to treat you in a more grown up way. After you have been doing this for a few weeks, point it out to them. Don't be surprised if nothing happens right away. Try to be patient.

10 My parents are always butting into my private life. I'm angry that they don't trust me. How can I get them to but out of my private life?

Often, teenagers assert their independence by not letting their parents into their lives. Instead of pushing them away, try to understand where they are coming from. They love you very much, and when they hear all the terrible things that happen to other teenagers, they can't help being frightened that something awful could happen to you too.

As you were growing up, you often went to them for comfort and reassurance when something scared you. Now they need reassurance that they have raised you to know how to take care of yourself and stay out of trouble. You can give them this reassurance by talking to them about your life. Talk, talk, talk until they are tired of listening! Talk to your parents about your friends, about what is happening at school, about what you think about drugs, drinking, about sex and pregnancy. If you let them know what is going on in your life and what you think, they may relax when they feel that they can trust you more. You may even be surprised to find out that they can actually make helpful suggestions. They too were once teenagers and faced many of the same problems that you do.

Some parents never trust their children, even when they are fully grown. Some parents are more protective of their daughters than of their sons. If you feel frustrated after you have tried some of these suggestions, talk to an older person you trust: an older friend, relative, teacher, school counsellor or minister.[1]

11 Why won't my parents let me date?

As with other adult freedoms, being allowed to date is a matter of gaining your parents' trust. Trust is not something you automatically deserve; it is something you earn. How hard have you been working on building up trust between you and your parents lately? In the last two questions, we discussed some of the ways you can build up trust and show your parents you are ready for more independence.

If you are not dating, don't feel bad. There really isn't as much dating going on as you may think, even in high school. Most of the dates you hear about are just talk. It is just too expensive for a couple to date a lot. Of course as you get older, there is more and more socializing and partying with young people of the opposite sex.

12 What do you think about dating?

There is not as much dating going on as most people think. There is a great deal of getting together, hanging out and casual meeting, but not a lot of so-called dating. It is expensive, and teenagers often have higher standards for what a date should be than what they can really live up to. Many feel they need to use a car, buy new clothes and go to someplace expensive. If you have ever given a party, you know how much snacks and pop alone may cost.

There is one aspect of dating that is very common: date rape. This often happens when a young man feels he is entitled to have sex with a girl as payment for the ten, fifteen or twenty dollars he has spent on the evening out. So he may pressure the girl. Some girls find it hard to resist such an approach, as they too feel that they owe something for the evening out. Or, the boy may simply force himself on the girl. Any young man who has this attitude about dating is degrading his companion and treating her as though she were a prostitute. Intercourse is part of an intimate relationship; each person has the right to decide for him- or herself when to have sex. It is not something to be treated as something given in payment for favors.

13 Why are my parents so mean to me?

The basic reason is fear. Have you ever noticed that when a person has had a scare, he or she often covers it up by getting angry? You may have done this yourself. You may have worried about someone or something and when it is all over, you let out your feelings of worry by getting angry.

Your parents may simply be afraid because they constantly hear about many bad things happening to teenagers. They may get angry at you because they are afraid something might happen to you if they don't exercise control over you. This is discussed more fully in the previous two questions.

But sometimes, when we are worried or frightened because things are not going right in our lives, we look for someone else to blame for our troubles. This may be what your parents are doing when they get angry at you. Having a family is a big responsibility and your parents may be worried about money, about their jobs or about the future. We expect our parents to always treat us fairly, but they are not perfect, and sometimes they act unfairly. If you think this is happening, wait until they are not angry at you, and let them know in a calm voice that you think they often get angry with you for no reason. You can also try to figure out what is bothering them—or even ask them—and let them know that you are concerned too.

14 What can I do about my uncle touching me when I don't like it?

It is very important for you to realize that no one has the right to touch you in ways that you don't like. Often we don't like to be hugged or kissed by certain people, or we dislike the way they hug and kiss us. Sometimes it seems too personal or sexual. We only like to be touched on our private parts by our husbands or wives, boyfriends or girlfriends, and even then not all of the time!

If someone in the family is doing this to you, it may take some effort to get them to stop. But you have a right to feel comfortable among your own family members. You can begin by telling the person to stop, and how it makes you feel when he or she touches you. You can say, "I like you, but I don't want to be hugged or touched that way," or "Please don't do that. It makes me feel very uncomfortable." If they don't stop, you should talk to your mother or father about it.

If someone has been touching your private parts, it is a very serious matter. You should **begin** by talking to a member of your family who is not doing the touching. If family members don't seem willing to help, you should talk to a trusted teacher, school counsellor or minister. As a last resort, you may have to contact the police department's sex crimes unit. Remember, it is not only wrong, it is against the law for someone to touch your private parts without your permission. If you are a minor and the other person is an adult it is against the law for the adult to touch you even with your permission.

15 If you "do it" with someone in your family, can you get pregnant?

You certainly can. Having intercourse with someone in your family is called incest. It is against the law. It is also illegal for an adult to have intercourse with a child. When this happens, it is never the fault of the child, no matter how "sexy" the child may appear to act. Adults are entrusted with the care of their children, and they violate that trust when they have sex with their own or other children. This is a form of sexual molestation. If you know a child or teenager whom you think is having intercourse with someone in his or her family, you should tell your teacher, your school counsellor or your parents about it. If they don't help, you should go to the police.

B. EMERGING SEXUAL IDENTITY

16 Why does Mary always have to wear a skirt?

I don't know why Mary always wears a skirt to school. Maybe she likes to wear skirts. Maybe she doesn't have any slacks to wear to school. Maybe her mother thinks that girls should always wear skirts. Girls used to always have to wear skirts to school. Perhaps you should ask her why.

If you get to be friends with Mary, maybe it won't matter what she wears. It is all right to be different. In fact, it's fun to be different from everyone else. Is there something you have never done that is a little different and that you would like to try? Life gets boring when we do the same things the same way all of the time.

17 Why do kids use "dirty" words?

These words that we call "dirty" are also called "swear" words. When people are angry or upset, they sometimes use these words to show their anger. Sometimes they use them to tease or to make other people uncomfortable. Often, kids use them even though they don't even know what they mean. They have heard someone else use them, and so they think these words are all right to use.

Small children may use them because they have found that they can get a reaction from adults that way. It is helpful to tell a small child what the word means and let him/her decide whether to continue using it. It is a good idea to notice what "dirty" words you use in your conversation and to try to get rid of them. They have a way of slipping out at the wrong time and embarrassing you.

18 Why are some boys so mean? Why are boys meaner than girls?

Some boys and some girls are mean. This is because someone has been mean to them and they think that this is the way to act. Sometimes these same boys and girls really want to be friendly, but they don't know how. Sometimes they act mean because they want to impress their friends and don't care whom they hurt.

Learning how to make and keep friends is important both now and later. It's important now because you can be very lonely without good friends. It will be important in adult life because a central part of marriage is friendship between husband and wife. Sexual attraction is usually not enough to make a marriage last.

19 During gym class at school, I feel uncomfortable changing clothes in front of lots of people in the locker room. Is this normal?

Privacy is something we all like to have when we are dressing. It is normal to feel uncomfortable when changing clothes with many other people. But gym classes are so large that privacy is not possible. It is especially hard for a girl or boy if other children are making fun of their bodies. If you hear others teasing someone for being too short or too tall, too thin or too fat, tell the teasers to knock it off. If this doesn't work, it is not wrong to tell the teacher so that he or she can put an end to it.

We all have our own schedule for growing up. No one can control when a boy first grows pubic hair or a girl begins to develop breasts. Some people develop and change early, some later. People who tease others show that **they** are the childish ones, no matter how they may look on the outside. Remember the story of the ugly duckling who changed into a beautiful swan!

20 What is the best way to handle teasing?

People who tease are usually trying to "get" to you. They are looking for something that they know you are uncomfortable about and that will upset you. If you ignore their teasing, often they will see that it doesn't bother you, and they will stop doing it. If they don't, tell them that teasing is a childish way to act. (Also, see the previous question and answer.)

21 When can I begin wearing a bra, long stockings, etc.?

Different parents have different ideas about this. Some parents don't want to see their girls grow up too soon so they don't give them permission to wear these clothes as early as the girl would like.

Girls do not need a bra when their breasts are first beginning to develop. There are strong muscles that support the breasts at first. Later, when they are more fully developed, the bra is used to help keep the breasts from bouncing up and down. This can be a special problem for girls and women who are very active. If a bra will make you feel more comfortable, ask your mother for one. Perhaps your mother does not know that this is important to you and you may need to remind her several times about it. If it is really important to you to be dressed as your friends are, perhaps you can offer to save your own money for these items.

22 Why do people engage in prostitution?

We don't always know. Some people think that it is an easy way to make a lot of money. Some, usually women, think that they are not qualified to do any other kind of work. Some people are foolish enough to think that, if you enjoy sex a lot, this is a good way to make money. But most prostitutes report no enjoyment of sex with the strangers who are paying them, and their "professional" life usually cripples their ability to form close personal relationships.

It is also a very dangerous way to live. Prostitutes can easily be mistreated, beaten or even murdered. They usually lose contact with their family and friends, so if they become sick, there is no one to help them. Prostitutes are especially likely to catch one or more kinds of sexually transmitted diseases. If you have intercourse with a prostitute, you too run a high risk of catching a sexually transmitted disease. Prostitutes are often involved in robbing their clients or harassing them in other ways. You cannot complain to the police, because being the customer of a prostitute is against the law in most areas.

23 What are homosexuals?

Homosexuals are people who love someone of the same sex instead of the opposite sex. It means that two men or two women are sexually attracted to each other, and are acting like husband and wife. We are told that about one adult in ten is a homosexual.

Right now, people disagree about whether homosexuality is something that should be accepted or condemned. We don't know much about why or how some people become attracted to members of the same sex.

It is normal for two boys or two girls to like each other a lot and become close friends. This does not mean that they are homosexuals. If you have one or more close friends of the same sex, you don't have to worry about being a homosexual. Some teenagers don't start dating until they are eighteen or nineteen years old. They may be involved in other activities during these years. This is quite normal, and doesn't mean they are homosexual. If you or someone you know is worried or afraid that you might be a homosexual, talk to a parent, teacher, school counsellor, minister or some other adult you trust.[2]

24 What are "fags," "queers," "homos," "lessies," "gays?"

These are slang terms for homosexuals. "Lessie" is short for "lesbian," which is the term for a female homosexual. Today most homosexuals prefer to be called "gay." The words "fag," "queer," and "homo," are derogatory and insulting terms for homosexuals. People use them because they think that being sexually attracted to the same sex is strange or sick. This is because most people are heterosexual, which means they are attracted to members of the opposite sex.

Most children and teenagers are very sensitive about being made to feel different or "weird." Calling someone a "homo," a "fag" or a "queer" is a very bad thing to do, because it can upset him or her very much, and make that person feel that there is something very "wrong" with him or her.

25 How does a homosexual become what he is?

We really don't know. There are several theories about why people turn out to be homosexual, but none of them are universally accepted. One theory is that the person got turned off to people of the opposite sex as a child—perhaps because a family member of the opposite sex treated the person harshly. But in most cases, this has turned out not to be true. Homosexuals seem to have received the same treatment in their families as their brothers and sisters. Another theory is that these people have a different chemical make-up than other people. This also has yet to be demonstrated. Most recently, there is a theory that the mothers of homosexuals were under extreme stress or took drugs during the pregnancy, and that this changed the hormonal make-up of the baby in some way. But so far little evidence has been found to confirm this theory. We just do not know why a person turns out to be homosexual.

26 Can you tell a homosexual by his looks?

No, you cannot. It used to be thought that a man must be a homosexual if he looked or acted somewhat feminine. It was thought that a woman must be a lesbian if she looked and acted somewhat masculine. This caused much unhappiness for people who were labelled in this way. Now we know better.

People cannot do much about how they look. They may not look totally masculine or totally feminine because of the hormone balance in their bodies. If a man has a great deal of the male hormone and little female hormone in his body he will look very masculine. If he has a more even balance of male and female hormone, he may look somewhat more feminine. Perhaps he grows tall and has a thick beard, but a softer and higher voice. The reverse is true for women.

But most of these people are not homosexuals. They fall in love with a member of the opposite sex, marry, have children—in short, they lead normal, heterosexual lives.

Some teenagers do not finish their growing until they are in their late teens or early twenties. They may not look either very masculine or very feminine until they finish their growing. It is thoughtless and childish to label people homosexuals simply because they do not live up to our expectations of how they should look. The only way you can tell that a person is homosexual is either because they tell you or by their explicit sexual behavior.

27 Do men ever marry other men?

Some homosexual couples consider themselves to be married. Although the government doesn't recognize such "marriages," some states are beginning to treat homosexual couples more like married couples.

Often two or more men or women live together as roommates to share expenses of food and housing. This is very common and does not have anything to do with whether they are homosexuals or not.

28 Can homosexuals have sex?

They can have many forms of sexual activity. They can hug and kiss in a sexual way, just like anyone else. Two men can have anal intercourse. Female homosexuals cannot, of course, have intercourse, so they have sex by touching each other's vaginas with their hands as well as oral sex (see Glossary).

29 What is a whore or prostitute?

A whore or prostitute is a person, usually but not always female, who has sex with people for money.

The word "whore" can also be used to insult someone who has sex with many different partners. Whether this is good or not is a very difficult question to answer, but calling someone a whore is usually just a way of teasing someone. Being called a whore usually doesn't mean that the whole school thinks that you may be having sex with your boyfriend. It should be treated like other forms of teasing; if you show that it doesn't bother you, usually the teasers will stop.

C. SEXUAL EXPRESSION AND SEXUAL RELATIONSHIPS

30 Why do people kiss?

Kissing is a way of showing a person that you like him or her, like hugging or shaking hands. Shaking hands is a way of showing people we like and trust them. Hugging and kissing are ways of showing people we not only like and trust them, but that we like them a lot or even love them.

There are several different kinds of kissing. Public kisses are usually short, and are ways that people may show they like or love each other. Private kisses usually last longer and express stronger feelings like love. "Open mouth" kisses are private kisses.

Public kisses are fine when other people are around. But when people give each other private kisses in public, it can make other people uncomfortable or embarrassed. Perhaps you have felt uncomfortable when you have seen other people giving private kisses in public. Often you may see private kissing on T.V. If this makes you uncomfortable you can watch something else.

31 If a boy doesn't have a girlfriend, why does he become "horny?"

Being "horny" means that one is having sexual feelings. People can have these feelings just from thinking about a member of the opposite sex—even someone they don't know or have only seen in a picture or on T.V. The most powerful sexual organ of the body is not the penis or the vagina—it is the brain! If you choose to think about sexual activities, you may feel "horny." With the vast amount of often very explicit sexual activity now shown on T.V. and in movies, it is not surprising that many teenagers often find themselves thinking sexual thoughts or having sexual phantasies. But there is a control for this. You can choose to think about other things some of the time. You can choose what you watch on T.V. and how much you watch. You can get involved in other activities. But there is nothing wrong with thinking about sex or having sexual fantasies. Indeed, it is very pleasurable!

32 Why do teenage boys like having sex with teenage girls?

The drive to have sex is very strong in teenagers, probably stronger in teenage boys. But there is more to it than that. Some boys want to do it as much to impress their friends as because of their real desires. They may do it to be able to tell their friends—or they may brag they are doing it with someone when they really aren't. They also may do it to feel grown up. They put intercourse in the same category as smoking or learning to drive a car: it's a way of reassuring themselves that they are no longer really children.

Many boys who have intercourse still have a rather childish attitude about sex. They feel that pregnancy is only the girl's responsibility. They think that "if she's dumb enough to trust me, then it's her problem, not mine." Of course, if the girl really does become pregnant, many teenage boys realize just how serious a matter it is. Until then, they think of intercourse as a game, and like to see how often they can "score." Many boys do not share this attitude, but some do.

33 Why do people sometimes say that I can't touch myself?

We all have public places and private places on our bodies. It is all right to touch the public places of your body any time—your face, your hands, your hair and so forth. It is all right to touch your privates—such as the area between your legs—when you are in a private place such as your own bedroom or the bathroom by yourself.

Many people get upset if they see someone touching their privates in public. It is also not a good idea to talk about touching yourself to just anyone you know. If you want to talk about it, speak to your parents, a teacher you are close to or your doctor. (See "Masturbation" in the Glossary.)

34 Is it good to masturbate? Can you do it too often?

It is all right to touch any part of your body, including your private parts. There is no harm in masturbating, but it should be done in private, usually in your own bedroom. It is very private and just for you. It is fine to do things that are just for you alone.

Masturbation does not harm a person. In a society where we are exposed to much more sexual stimulation than we can ever hope to satisfy with a partner, it is an appropriate form of sexual pleasure and release. It is also quite ancient and was mentioned as a common practice in learned writings at least five hundred years ago.

Ideas about masturbation have changed a lot. It used to be thought that masturbation could cause bodily damage, or make the person insane or blind. Now we know that this is totally false.

You cannot masturbate too often. In boys and men, after an ejaculation, the penis will not become firm for a short period of time. The male body seems to need this recovery period. But if you feel that you are masturbating too much, then it is probably too much for you. If you feel OK about how much you masturbate, then this is probably OK for you. The only time you might be masturbating too much is when it keeps you from doing other things you want to do or you know that you should do, such as having a social life with friends, helping around the house, or doing school work.

But masturbation, like other forms of sexual activity, must be done in private. Many people find it extremely offensive to have to see someone else doing it, so there are laws against masturbation or exposing one's sexual organs in public.

If you feel guilty about masturbation, or worry about it, try to talk about it with your parents, school counsellor, doctor, minister or some other adult you trust.[3]

35 Is it all right for a girl to masturbate?

Female masturbation is not harmful and quite common. It involves stroking the vagina and the clitoris. See Question 34 above.

36 If a guy masturbates a lot, will he still be able to father children in the future?

Yes. A man's body produces millions and millions of sperm every day. It replaces very quickly those sperm which are ejaculated. A male produces sperm every day from the time of sexual maturity until the day he dies. It used to be thought that a man had a certain, fixed amount of sperm, and that if he wasted it by masturbation he would not have enough left to have children later. Now we know that this is a myth. Indeed, now and then the male body gets rid of excess sperm in the middle of the night. This is called a "nocturnal emission," or a "wet dream," because it is often accompanied by a sexy dream.

Some forms of sexually transmitted disease, if not cleared up early, can damage a boy's ability to father children. But masturbation cannot.

37 Why do some boys like to look at the pictures of naked women?

Both some girls and some boys like to look at pictures of men and women who do not have any clothes on. Often they are curious to see what people of the opposite sex look like when they are naked. There are special magazines that show women and men naked.

It is normal to enjoy looking at naked people. The human body is very beautiful, and many great artists have painted pictures or made statues of people who are nude. It is OK to do this if you want to, and it is just as OK not to do this. But this is something that you should not do at school or when a lot of other people are around, as it would probably make them very uncomfortable. Also, some magazines show pictures of naked men and women chained up or being hurt. They give people the wrong idea that hurting someone or being hurt is a normal part of sex. It is not normal and such magazines should be avoided.

38 Can children have sexual intercourse?

Sexual intercourse is for grown-up people. You should not let anyone have intercourse with you now, as it would most likely be very upsetting to you for a long time. If you think someone wants to have intercourse with you now when you are a child, you should say no, go away from that person, and tell your parents, teachers, or another grown-up you trust right away. If someone touches you in a private place that you don't like, don't be afraid to say no. If that person is much older than you, tell your parents, teachers, or another grown-up you trust right away. If you think that the person won't like you for saying no, remember that a real friend would not try to make you do something you don't want to.

39 What happens when a teenage girl becomes pregnant?

When a teenage girl begins to suspect that she is pregnant, it is best for her to go to a clinic or doctor as soon as possible for a pregnancy test. If she has had intercourse and missed her next period, she probably is pregnant, although there are other reasons her period may be late.

If she is pregnant, she finds herself faced with many decisions. Because she will soon need a great deal of help and support, it is usually a good idea for her to tell her parents and the father. She will need to consider whether she wants to keep her baby, give it up for adoption or have an abortion. (The decision to abort the baby needs to be made very early, as many clinics or doctors will not perform an abortion after twelve weeks. Abortions may be quite costly as well, if this procedure is not covered by the girl's medical insurance.)

These are all very difficult decisions. Because her family and friends may all have very strong feelings about what she should do, she ought to seek counseling from someone who is not directly involved. A counsellor will help her think through her decisions, and to distinguish what she wants from what others think is "best" for her.

If she decides to carry the baby, she needs to begin prenatal care early. The baby's health may depend on her receiving early and continuing medical care. For one thing, sexually transmitted diseases can severely damage the baby, unless cleared up immediately. Each community is different in the services it offers. Some may have free clinics; others may charge a fee based on their patients' ability to pay.

A big problem is housing. Do she and the child's father wish to marry and establish a home together? Can she continue to live with her family? Some parents can help their daughter, some cannot or will not. Can she live with a relative or friend? If both her family and the baby's father refuse to help her, how will she support herself? Some forms of financial support available are general assistance, Aid to Dependent Children and Medicare. Information and help can often be obtained from the city or county Department of Social Services and Department of Public Health. However, public assistance is usually only enough to maintain the bare necessities of life—if that much.

If she finds a job, who will care for the child? Some communities have free or low-cost childcare facilities, others do not.

How will she finish her schooling? Can she continue to attend classes or are there special classes she can attend until the baby is born?

Finally, who will help the mother take care of the child? A small child is a heavy, never-ending responsibility and is extremely difficult for a teenage girl.

Here are six common myths about having a child:

1. It will make your friends respect you more.
2. It will make you appear more grown up.
3. A baby is capable of loving you as soon as it is born.
4. A baby is a cute, cuddly creature that just couldn't be that hard to take care of.
5. It will help cement your relationship with your boyfriend.
6. It will solve all of your problems.

40 What are the problems a teenager with a baby faces when she lives with her parents?

If a teenage mother lives at home with her parents and her new baby, life may become very difficult. A teenager may think that by having her own child she will be treated as an independent adult. Instead, she may find that she is not able to act as mother to her own baby. Her mother and father—the baby's grandmother and grandfather—take over and act as mother and father to the baby because they have had more experience. This is difficult for the real mother to resist, especially since her parents are supporting her and the baby.

If the girl is old enough to get a full-time job and be on her own, she may still find that she needs her own parents to take care of the baby while she works. Professional child care is often very expensive and usually a woman just beginning to work full-time is not able to afford it. She will find herself with two full-time jobs: the one she works at all day, and caring for her child when she is at home. Whether the new mother lives with her parents or by herself, there will probably not be enough money to pay for everything the mother and the baby need.

41 What are the father's responsibilities to the child? When a father just "takes off" and abandons the mother and child, what happens?

The father is required to contribute to the child's support until the child reaches the age of eighteen years. If he does not, the mother can go to the county court and ask the court to force him to contribute. The court decides the amount. This amount increases as the father grows up and his income increases. Support payments must continue until the child is eighteen years of age. The court can require his employer to take the money out of his paycheck or seize his property, even if he moves to another state. This could damage his credit and make it hard for him to get auto or housing loans.

However, sometimes if the father moves away it is difficult to locate him. Some courts will keep after the father until they find him; some will not, especially if they are under-staffed. Even if the teenage father is living nearby, he will probably have no job, income or property. Then he cannot be made to contribute until he starts working.

The young man may also deny he is the father. Although scientific tests may prove the truth, they are difficult and expensive to perform.

42 Why do some teenagers have babies when they are not married?

Most unmarried teenage girls don't want to get pregnant. There are many misconceptions about pregnancy. A girl may get pregnant because she and her boyfriend don't realize how easy it is to do so. They think that pregnancy won't happen to her, or that it can't happen the first time the girl has sex. Some boys and girls don't realize that even a ten-year-old girl can have a baby.

Sometimes a girl doesn't know how to tell if she is pregnant, and it is only several months later that she becomes aware of it. Then it is too late to decide whether or not to have the baby.

Sometimes the parents of one or both members of a couple work full time, and teenagers have many opportunities to be alone together in private. They use this privacy to become sexually involved.

Sometimes the couple tries to use a birth control method, but they don't know how to use it properly. Sometimes a boy may feel that he must appear to know how to use a condom even when he doesn't, and his girlfriend accepts his word.

Sometimes teenage girls and boys find it difficult to talk about their sexual feelings with each other, or even admit them to themselves. Some girls are afraid to say "no" to their boyfriends, and fear that they will lose them if they don't give in. Their boyfriends don't recognize how much it will hurt their girlfriends if they become pregnant.

Often, a boy and girl do not admit to each other or even to themselves that they want to "go all the way," and so they are not prepared when their feelings become strong. Each may feel that the other will think less of her or him if she or he is prepared with birth control. Each may feel that if he or she admits to wanting to have intercourse, it makes him or her an immoral person. This is especially true for a girl, who may be labelled a "whore" or "tramp" by foolish "friends." So if intercourse just "happens" without any planning, both partners can tell themselves they didn't "really" want to do it.

Common to most of these difficulties is a failure to understand the strength of sexual feelings and how they can weaken your judgment and common sense. Boys and girls need to talk about their feelings before they get into a situation where the feelings may take charge. A girl should not feel that she alone is responsible for not getting pregnant. In the next few questions, we will discuss how these feelings operate and how you can control them. For information on birth control, see the chapter on birth control.

43 What is the sex drive?

There are many kinds of drives. Some people are driven to achieve security by earning and saving money. Some are driven to achieve power in business or politics. Some people are driven to help other people. In teenagers, it is common to have a strong drive to finish school, to get more education, to be popular, even just to have fun.

Sex is a very powerful drive, more powerful than any other drive you have experienced. It comes from the basic need of the human species to reproduce. But people do not have intercourse only to have children. We also have intercourse to feel close to someone we care about, or just because it feels pleasurable.

We all have the ability to feel powerfully attracted to someone else. People have been experiencing this feeling since the human race began. It can add much enjoyment to life, and bring you closer to someone you like and know well.

But sex and pregnancy can also disrupt other plans, like pursuing further education or a career. Any drive can disrupt your life if you let it take control of you: the desire for money can take over so that you are incapable of having fun with your friends. The overwhelming desire to excel in sports can keep you from doing well in school. Like other drives, sex can disrupt your education, interfere with your work and weaken other friendships if you don't use your head to control it. Sexual activity may, of course, lead to unwanted pregnancies. But you also need to remember that sexual activity usually has a strong emotional impact on you. If you engage in sex with people whom you have not gotten to know very well, you may get badly hurt. That is why it is important to understand the sex drive and learn how to manage it.

44 Why is sex called a "drive" and not an "instinct?" Aren't they the same thing?

No. An instinct is a pattern of behavior built into an animal from birth. Animals operate on instinct for the most part. When a young bird falls or is pushed from the nest, it flaps its wings by instinct. It has never been taught how to move its wings. Instincts help animals survive even though most of them have little ability to reason and think about how to find food and shelter. We humans have instincts too—our hearts beat faster when we are in danger.

Mostly humans act out of drives. We experience these drives as strong emotions that press us to do something. These drives do not dictate a specific pattern of behavior.

Drives are more easily molded and redirected than instincts. Anything you feel strongly about trying to accomplish is a drive for you: wanting to finish school, wanting to play the guitar well or wanting to be a good baseball player are all familiar drives.

We use our reason and experience to mold and direct our drives. For example, the drive to eat can be satisfied in many different ways—through cooking many different kinds of food. We can also restrict it so that we eat less than we want to. We can also postpone it so that if we are hungry while driving on the highway, we do not forget about driving the car and immediately start eating or looking for food. A baby has not yet learned this kind of control—when it is hungry, that is all it focuses on. As soon as it is hungry, the baby starts to cry until it is fed.

Mating in animals is an instinct. Although mating rituals in animals may be quite complex, they all follow patterns built into their bodily structures. When a peacock unfolds its beautiful feathers to attract the peahen, this is not something it has thought of by itself! The peacock uses his spread of feathers to drive the peahen into the nest. This is **instinctive.**

For human beings, mating is not something your nature compels you to do, like breathing. It is something that you have a strong drive to do. This drive appears both in the person's feelings and in the body. Because it is a drive, and not an instinct, you can use your reason to choose when to follow it and when not to. Just as with any other drive, a number of choices are available to you when you experience the sex drive. You can choose to manage and control the feelings of sexual arousal so that they will give you enjoyment, not problems. Or you can choose to get all the sexual pleasure you can without thinking about the consequences for yourself or your partner. Then, you are acting more like an animal, and less like a human being.

45 Does intercourse hurt?

No, not if the man and the woman are grown up. It could hurt a young girl, as her body is not yet finished growing and her vagina is still very small. It can also hurt if the girl has mixed feelings about having intercourse. Then the muscles of her vagina may become tense and make intercourse uncomfortable or painful. If you are finding intercourse painful, this is a message that something may be wrong with your relationship. You need to postpone having sex for awhile and do some serious thinking about how you and your boyfriend really feel about having sex with each other.

46 Does a person have to have sex? My boyfriend says he has to have intercourse, otherwise he says he feels pain or becomes very emotionally upset.

It may sometimes seem to someone that he or she has to have sexual intercourse. This gives you a sense of how strong the sex drive can become in a person's life. You may even have felt that you must have intercourse to have sexual release. The truth is, no one ever died from not having sexual intercourse when he or she wanted it very much. If you and your partner separate for a little while, the sexual tension will gradually decline. It can be very uncomfortable for a couple of hours, but it can and does drain away. Masturbation may also provide sexual release for both men and women.

When someone tells you that he (or she) has to have intercourse, what they are really saying is simply, "I want it." Wanting something very much is not the same thing as needing it.

47 Can you have sex and still remain a virgin?

No. You can't have it both ways. There are many times when we would like two opposite things. We want a lot of money but we don't want to work very hard. We want good grades but we don't want to spend hours studying. A virgin is a person who has never had sexual intercourse.

Once you have intercourse, you are no longer a virgin. Although there is a book out called "How To Become A Virgin," it is not possible to return to a state of virginity after you have had intercourse!

There is nothing wrong with wanting to have intercourse with someone. We all have this marvelous ability to fall in love and to be attracted to someone of the opposite sex. But desiring something does not mean that you have to do it. You may choose to or you may choose not to.

For example, you may feel that it is important to save the experience of having intercourse for the person you marry. This is a very legitimate feeling. Virginity is a very lovely gift that you can give someone you love. This decision is a very difficult one. Perhaps you would benefit from talking it over with someone whom you trust: your parents, a grown up relative, your school counsellor or your minister.

48 Does sexual intercourse feel good?

It usually feels very good at the time it is happening. Later on, the person may have some very negative feelings about it. These feelings deserve to be taken very seriously; they are telling the person that his/her sexual activity may bring a lot of problems.

Some girls say that they don't feel any pleasure during intercourse, and they wonder what all the excitement is about. There can be many reasons for this lack of pleasure. Sometimes a girl comes from a very strict family that has told her that sex is completely wrong and sinful, and that sexual feelings only happen to bad people.

But more often, this lack of enjoyment is caused by anxiety and worry. They are anxious and tense because of something about the situation. The girl may feel that the relationship is not very secure or that the boy does not care very deeply for her. People who are deeply committed to each other and trust each other are more likely to experience great pleasure and enjoyment from sex with each other. Many teenagers over-look these emotional factors, and can't understand why sex for them is not what it's cracked up to be.

49 How can I control my sex drive?

The power of the sex drive can be very confusing to you. You may think, "I feel so strongly that I want to do this, it must be right for me." But what you feel strongly that you want and what you know is the right thing for you are often not at all the same thing. If you see a shiny red sports car that you want to own, your reason tells you that you can't just take it, and that this is a desire that you will have to postpone or put aside. Your reason reminds you of the consequences of taking someone else's car.

When you have a strong sexual desire, you also need to allow your reason to remind you of the possible consequences. Telling yourself that "if it feels good, it must be right," makes no more sense here than it does in "borrowing" an exciting sports car that doesn't belong to you.

To exercise control over your sexual feelings, it is important to understand how they operate.

50 How does the sex drive operate?

When you are attracted to another, you experience a rising tension and excitement of the emotions and of the body. This is also called being "turned on" or "getting hot."

You can get turned on by other things than sex. Some people get turned on by music—just listening makes them feel good all over. Other people get turned on by sports, especially when they are in a competitive situation. Many people engage in strenuous physical activity like tennis, jogging or bicycle riding because it makes them feel good. When they are finished, they feel good all over, even though they may be very tired.

The sex drive is very similar, except that you don't need intense physical activity to get turned on. Your body can respond powerfully when you see someone attractive to you, when you kiss, touch or even when you are just thinking about sex. You may begin to feel good all over. Your heart may speed up and your breathing may become heavier and more rapid. The blood comes to the surface of the skin and makes you feel hot. You begin to perspire more.

After a short period of intense kissing, your body may go "on alert." Adrenalin is poured into the blood stream to assist the body in its turned on condition. If you have been involved in competitive sports, you may have experienced this "alert." If you play hard enough to use most of your available energy, you often experience a "second wind." This happens because adrenalin is entering your blood stream to give you a new surge of energy.

In sports, the adrenalin is quickly used up. But when you are sexually excited, it isn't. Instead, it travels through the blood to the brain. There, adrenalin can alter your thinking. Most of the time, you may know that you do not want to have intercourse because of the risks to you of pregnancy, hurt feelings and venereal diseases. But when your thinking is altered by sexual excitement, you are likely to begin thinking differently. Now you are thinking that you will risk intercourse just this once, that you will be lucky, that nothing bad will happen to you.

How do you control the sex drive? First, you recognize how powerful it is, and that when you get really turned on, it may alter your thinking. You keep reminding yourself that if you are sexually turned on for too long you may lose your ability to think clearly about sexual issues. You remember that you want to be in control of your life and your sex drive; you do not want it to control you.

Second, you learn to recognize the signs of being turned on, both in yourself and in the other person: the rapid heart beat, the heavy breathing, the warm feeling.

Third, you interrupt your sexual activity before your thinking has been clouded. If you separate or "change the subject" for awhile, you will decrease the tension and excitement. Then the sexual emotions and sexual feelings in the body will subside. You may say that you are hungry or thirsty. Or you might say that you are expected home in fifteen minutes. But it is not easy to stop when you are enjoying sex so much. You might also plan the date so that only a limited time will be available for sexual activity.[4]

51 Is it all right to pet?

This is a difficult question to answer. Petting refers to sexual touching below the neck—usually to touching the breasts or penis or vagina, often under the clothing. Petting can arouse very strong sexual feelings, and especially the desire to have intercourse. It is best for a boy and girl who care for each other to think ahead of time about "how far" they are going to go.

If you are a girl, you probably know that if you "go all the way" you may become pregnant. But if you are a boy, you too should realize that pregnancy is a very real possibility. If you only think about "how far you can get," you may wind up getting your girlfriend pregnant.

Sexual feelings must be managed so that they don't get out of control. The partners in a couple need to make definite decisions, either together or alone, about how far they want to go. If you engage in sexual activity for more than about twenty minutes, the sexual excitement and tension can become very strong. The couple may have intercourse while they are experiencing these strong sexual feelings, even though they really didn't intend to or want to. Often a teenager has said to me, "I don't know what happened to me; I just didn't want to stop."

You and your partner need to understand how easy it is to get "carried away" with the excitement of the moment. To avoid going further than you intend, you need to be able to tell when you are very turned on. You will know this is happening when you feel your heart beating faster, you notice you are breathing faster and you are experiencing strong feelings in your sexual organs. Something called "tunnel vision" often develops. This means that your sexual feelings are so strong that you only "see" one thing: your sexual feelings. You may forget about everything else. It's not that you cannot stop petting; it's that you are finding it so pleasurable that you don't **want** to stop. At this point, you will find it very difficult to think about pregnancy, sexually transmitted diseases or how you will feel about what you did the next day.

It is better to think ahead of time about how far you are going, than to just leave it to the spur of the moment. Often it is difficult for a teenage girl and boy to discuss sex with each other, but if you are frank and honest you will enjoy each other's company more, including sexual activity, and have less anxiety about getting pregnant or feeling pressured to do something that you do not want to. If you are a boy, your girlfriend will appreciate your willingness to take responsibility for not getting her pregnant. She will be relieved to find that she doesn't have to always be anxious and on guard to "fight you off" when necking or petting. If you are a girl, your boyfriend will be pleasantly surprised if you tell him frankly that you enjoy sexual touching, but want to set strict limits so you don't have to worry about getting pregnant or doing things that you are not comfortable with.

52 Why do boys "finger fuck" girls?

This is a form of petting (see previous question). This form of petting is usually very exciting and enjoyable to both the boy and the girl.

A boy may also be doing this to see if the girl will let him "go all the way" and have intercourse. It is better for both partners to discuss this issue frankly than for the boy to sneakily try to arouse the girl to do more than she feels comfortable with.

53 How do I discourage a boy's roving hands without scaring him off? How can I say "no" to someone I like?

A girl may fear that if she says "no," she will lose her boyfriend. The boy may even encourage her to believe this. It is very hard to tell a person no, especially someone you love. You are risking losing them.

But what kind of friend only stays friends with you as long as you do what he wants? That is a very selfish and one-sided friendship. A boy who cares for you will respect what you want if you are assertive and firm. He won't keep pressuring you to do something that you don't want to do.

If you are afraid to say "no" to sex, try first saying no to less important things—for example to a movie you don't really want to see. It may also help to try out what you're going to say in front of a mirror.

It is best to use words that express your feelings. This is a gentler way to say no than just using the word "NO." Usually you begin with "I" to get your feelings across. You might say, "I like you a lot but that makes me very uncomfortable." Or you could say, "I'm afraid of what might happen." Or, "I don't want to go all the way. I'm scared. I like you, but I'm not ready for this." Even though you want to be gentle, it is important to speak with conviction. If you speak in a small voice, you may sound like you are not very sure of what you want. You may have to repeat yourself several times. Also remember that it is much harder to say "no" after you are sexually aroused. Then, your own sex drive is urging you to say "yes."

Sometimes, a boy too finds that a girl wants to have sex with him and he does not. This approach will work for boys too.

54 When a girl says "no" to petting or intercourse, how can I tell if she really means it, or just feels that she has to pretend not to want to?

It is wrong to assume that most girls "really" want to have sex, and that they are saying no because they feel it is shameful or unfeminine to want sex. When you are very aroused, it is easy to deceive yourself that the girl wants what you want. There are a lot of non-verbal messages involved. If the girl does not pull away from you, if her tone of voice is playful rather than angry, she may not want you to stop. But if she pulls away, if she is firm in her insistence, don't kid yourself that she wants to go further.

Above all, it is **never** right to use physical force, or to think that if a girl agrees to go out with you, she owes it to you to have sex. It is much better to err on the side of not going far enough than to push a girl further than she wants to go.

Even if she does go "all the way" willingly, this doesn't let you off the hook for what happens later. If she becomes pregnant because neither of you acted responsibly, you are as obligated to deal with the pregnancy as she is. If she later regrets having intercourse because she wasn't fully comfortable about it, you may lose her as a girlfriend and a friend. If you pretend that you love her when you don't, and she has sex with you, you have done a dishonest and selfish thing that can hurt the girl very deeply. Any boy who brags to you about how he tricked a girl into having sex with him is only showing that he is still emotionally a little child.

Rather than continually pressuring your girlfriend to go further, you should let her know that she must be frank with you about her sexual feelings, and that you will respect her **whatever** she says. If she says "no," you won't pressure her constantly to change her mind, and if she says "yes," you won't think she is a tramp or a slut.

It is often very hard for a boy to take "no" for an answer, because a "no" may make you feel that you are not masculine or sexy. As you become more mature, you will realize that there are many reasons why a girl who is very attracted to you may not want to have sex with you, and that it is not a condemnation of your masculinity. Of course, not every girl will find you attractive, just as you don't find every girl attractive.

55 How can you just have fun and talk without getting into sex every time you are with someone of the opposite sex?

It is good to take charge of the dating situation. It helps to have a planned activity for the date, and to allow only a limited amount of free time before it is time to go home. If you suggest or accept a date without a planned activity, this may give the other person the message that you welcome being alone with the person to have a lot of sexual contact.

Sometimes it is good to double-date so that there are more people to visit with and less privacy. Of course this can backfire if the other couple insists on necking and petting.

56 My boyfriend (girlfriend) never wants to talk or do something interesting; he (she) just wants to have sex. What can I do about this?

Often sexual activity is an escape for a boy and a girl who are afraid to talk to each other. Instead, they use sex to boost their egos. But having sex will not make you or your partner feel more secure. Learning to trust and communicate with someone special is much more significant and strengthening for your ego than just having sex.

If you want a different relationship with your partner, you need to be assertive about it. Insist upon going to interesting places and finding activities other than sex. Although many teenaged couples do not have much money to spend on dating, you both can be creative in finding inexpensive activities.

Some teenagers have trouble talking. They have not had much experience talking with someone of the opposite sex and quickly run out of things to say. It helps to think ahead of time about possible topics of conversation. For many teenagers, sports is a very comfortable topic. Anything that interests you will probably interest your date as well, especially if you get across **why** it's fascinating to you. It's also helpful to have a few conversation-starting questions ready, such as, "What's the best time you ever had in your life?" or "What are you planning to do on your vacation?" Then, try to be a good listener. This is a great asset on a date. Everyone likes to be listened to. We often spend our entire lives trying to find someone who will really listen to what we have to say.

If you do run out of things to say, don't get nervous. Silence is a part of getting to know someone too. You don't have to rush in to fill the vaccuum. If you don't worry about what to say next, before too long you or your date will think of something new to talk about.

After you have had several dates where you both went to a movie, a ballgame, played tennis or went swimming, you will have a fund of shared experiences to talk about.

57 How can you avoid sexual stimulation when you are out on a date?

You can't completely avoid sexual stimulation when out on a date with someone you like. Notice how often couples who like each other smile, laugh or kid around when they are together. Notice how often they find the chance to touch each other, hold hands, have their arms around each other, or playfully push each other around. This is all mildly sexually stimulating.

But how do you avoid more intense sexual stimulation on a date? Sometimes you can, sometimes you cannot. If you cannot, you can still learn to live with it. It may help to stay in public places, plan an activity for the date and set a time by which the date will end. You can allow some private time for intimate sexual contact, but if you limit this time you will have a much better chance of staying in control of the situation and of yourself.

58 Is it true that boys want to have sex more than girls do, and if so why?

Yes, it is probably true. This is not because girls have a weaker sex drive than boys; it is because they are more aware of the negative consequences. From the time a girl has her first period, she usually knows that if she has intercourse she can become pregnant. Although we may feel that both the boy and the girl must share the burdens if the girl becomes pregnant, it is easy for the boy to run away, while the girl of course cannot.

59 Why don't girls want anyone to know they have had sex, but boys brag about it?

There are two questions here. First, why are girls shy about discussing sex? The idea still exists that a girl who has had sexual intercourse before marriage is "damaged goods." This is a very old myth, but it has been declining over the last twenty-five years or so. Years ago, it was thought that a man could only be sure of avoiding venereal disease if he married a virgin. It was thought that it was the woman who brought the disease into the relationship. We know now that this is not true. Either the man or the woman can give the other a venereal disease. Back then, a family could arrange a better marriage for their daughter if they could guarantee her virginity.

There is still some value in being a virgin. A virgin doesn't have to worry about becoming pregnant before she is married or ready to have a child; he doesn't have to worry about sexually transmitted diseases; waiting to have your first sexual experience with your wife or husband is also a special gift to give someone you love.

Why do boys brag about sex? Some boys think that it somehow proves that they are grown up or mature. They think that doing things that adults do makes them adults too. It's a little like thinking that if you eat the same breakfast cereal as an Olympic champion, that makes you a champion too![5]

60 Why are boys always so pushy about wanting sex?

Some boys are pushy, some are not. Many of the "pushy" boys are into playing sexual games. They don't care much about the girls they are with; they just want to experience the excitement and pleasure of intercourse. If a girl won't "do it," they just drop her. Often they are trying to prove to their friends that they are grown up by having intercourse with as many girls as possible. When they are with a girl on a date, they are thinking more about the impression they will make on their male friends than about the girl. Of course, such behavior is really a rather childish and selfish kind of game playing. Perhaps they should find a different set of friends.

Some guys are just testing. They think that "good" girls will say no. Most people no longer think that a girl is "bad" if she has intercourse.

Some guys think that they are expected to try to go as far as they can, that girls won't like them if they don't try.

Some girls play sexual games by suggesting to a boy that they will have sex with him in order to get him interested.

Most teenagers very often run into game playing of one kind or another. Don't despair! There is someone out there who feels and thinks as you do. It will probably take some time, but you will find a person you can trust eventually.

61 Why do people feel that if you don't have sex, you are not an adult?

Some teenagers are in a hurry to grow up. They think that if they move into the world of adult actions, if they do things that adults do, then they are adults themselves. They think that having intercourse, smoking, drinking and using drugs all prove that they are mature adults. They think that by mimicking the appearance of someone, they can actually become like that person. It's as if someone thought that by putting on a Detroit Tigers uniform, he could become good enough to play for the Tigers!

What such people have not learned is that being an adult means being able to accept many responsibilities. It means being able to take total care of oneself, to have a full time job and to be accountable for all one's actions. Handling such responsibilities is something that teenagers are still in the process of learning. Adults have more freedom than teenagers in sexual matters and in drinking (drugs are of course illegal for everyone), because they are supposed to have mastered the responsibility for handling the consequences of their actions. As you know, even many adults have not grown up enough to act responsibly. Just as learning to become a good baseball player takes time and practice, so too does learning to become an adult. There are no easy shortcuts.

Have you ever noticed that some people want everyone else to do the same thing they are doing? If they are smoking, they try to put you down for not smoking. If they are having intercourse, they put you down for not doing it too. Often, they are uncomfortable or insecure with what they are doing, and their only real pleasure comes not from the smoking or the sex, but from impressing you and their other friends. If you are not impressed with their bragging, they get angry and try to make you feel bad.

If you have to deal with such a person, you can outmaneuver them a little by telling them a little "white lie"—that you have tried sex and didn't feel good about doing it now. That way, it's harder for them to act like they are more experienced and sophisticated than you. If you are firm and consistent in resisting their put-downs, they may finally leave you alone. If they don't, you may not want to hang out with them anymore.

62 Does having intercourse affect your personality?

In our society, intercourse is built up as being a fantastic experience. Indeed it can be under the right conditions. Often teenagers think that after having sex, their whole life will take on a new zest.

But many teenagers find intercourse a big disappointment. They don't feel much different, except that now they have to worry about pregnancy or sexually transmitted disease. They may also discover that it was less important to their partners than to themselves. Then they are usually very hurt.

Teenage relationships often are rather short-lived. When a relationship ends quickly, the boy or girl may regret that he or she did something so intimate with someone he or she didn't really feel all that close to. All of us have had the experience of doing something we wish we had not done. Sometimes it is hard to forget these experiences, and we can have a lot of regret. Casual sexual intercourse can be a big source for regrets later. You will have to decide this for yourself.

63 How do you know if a boy or girl likes you?

There is no easy answer to this question. He or she may let you know if they like you. He or she may want to spend a lot of time with you. He or she may talk to you often, walk with you in the hall or sit near you in class. He or she may try to find things that you both like to do together.

64 How can I tell if a boy or girl really likes me a lot, or if he (or she) is just "handing me a line," in order to have sex.

Some boys think sex and sexual intercourse is just a game, and don't act with much responsibility for the girl. A boy may tell a girl that he loves her because he thinks that this is what she wants to hear, and that then she will have intercourse with him. If she is fooled, she will most likely feel deeply hurt and used. It also happens, though less frequently, that a girl wants to have intercourse with a boy for some superficial reason, like impressing her friends, and that she does not have a strong attachment for the boy. It is not always easy to tell what someone's motives are; the other person may not be clear in his or her own mind as to what he or she wants. It is usually best not to rush into an intensely sexual relationship until you have gotten to know the other person well, and until you know what your own feelings for the other person are. You can judge a person's sincerity better after you have known him or her for six months to a year.

65 How do you tell a boy (girl) that you like him (her)?

It can be very frightening for you to show interest in a member of the opposite sex. Your friends may start to tease you. The person you are interested in may even tease you or respond in a hurtful way.

If you are friendly, easy to talk to and show your own feelings, you will make it easier for the other person to express his or her own feelings. It helps not to laugh at others when they do something that makes them look a little silly or stupid, like dropping their books or spilling their lunch. If you don't make other people feel embarrassed or awkward, others will be less afraid that you will make fun of them when they show you they like you.

66 How do you go about telling a boy (or girl) that you love him (or her)?

Love is a very complicated word. It can mean different things to different people. You can love your parents, your dog, your teacher, your new dress, your boyfriend. Of course here we are talking about some kind of romantic feeling. But love to the other person might not mean the same thing as it does to you. You could scare away the other person with that word. To him or her, it might mean going steady, romantic touching and other things he or she is not ready for yet.

It is better to try to discover what the feeling really is, instead of just calling it "love." The best way to do this is to get to know the other person gradually. How can you do this? You can be interested in what he or she says and does. Be a good listener. All of us like to be listened to. You can also talk about your interests, your likes and dislikes, to the other person. This will give the other person a chance to realize that he or she enjoys being with you, and it will also give you a chance to understand better your own feelings for her or him. It will give you both a chance to come to trust each other better.

Boys and girls can love just as adults can. But even for adults, the word "love" can be very confusing. So it is better not to use it until you understand very well what your feelings are.

67 How can I tell if I am really in love, or I'm just infatuated?

It is very difficult to tell in a short time. Sexual attraction between two people can be so strong that it feels like real love. When you really love someone, you care for that person's happiness and welfare, as well as feeling sexual attraction for them. Sometimes these both happen in a relationship, sometimes they do not. It is best to give yourself some time to let you and your partner get to know each other better. A year is not too long to wait until you are sure. At first, both you and your partner naturally start by "putting your best foot forward," because you want to impress each other with how nice you are. But after a year, you and your partner will have seen the bad as well as the good sides of each other. As you get to see each other's real selves, your love will either be strengthened or fade away.

Some personality traits can be strong obstacles to lasting love. Extreme anger, selfishness or poor use of money can kill love. A good sign of real love is that each person is willing to be flexible and allow the other to have his or her way part of the time. Another sign of love is mutual respect and support for each other's goals. You may outgrow a person who does not respect and support you in your immediate and long-term goals. In sexual activity, a strong sign of love is the willingness to not pressure your partner to do something he or she is not comfortable with.[6]

68 What do you think about having sex with someone you are not in love with?

Sex is not something you do like going to the movies, playing baseball or hanging out with your friends. It is part of a relationship with another person. Generally, you will feel something for that other person and often expect that he or she will return those positive feelings. And because intercourse is the way a new life is created, there are important responsibilities that go along with the sex act—responsibilities you or your partner can't easily walk away from (you may also catch sexually transmitted diseases this way). You may be deeply hurt if you find that the other person did not take the situation as seriously as you did. Sometimes, when you do something you regret, guilt feelings last a long time.

Using another person for acts of casual sex can make it harder to establish a meaningful relationship later with someone you really care for. Part of feeling good about yourself is putting a high value on the kind of person you are and what you believe in. Casual sex may lower your own self esteem as well as the opinions of others who know you.

69 How do you go about explaining to a boy who truly believes he loves you that intercourse before marriage is wrong?

This is a value conflict. You may truly believe that pre-marital intercourse is wrong, and he may not. You cannot change another person's values.

What you can ask is that the other person respect your values. You can tell the other person how you feel and to respect your feelings. If you emphasize your own feelings, you avoid condemning the other person's sincere beliefs. You are not saying that it is wrong for everyone, only that it is wrong for you and that you feel strongly about this issue.

It is important to speak firmly and to say what you feel repeatedly. This is called being assertive. Don't get upset if your partner doesn't seem to hear you the first few times, and don't give up getting your feelings across after one or a few attempts. If after asserting yourself about twenty times, the other person doesn't start respecting your wishes, you may have to face the fact that your ideas are too far apart for you to get along with each other. It doesn't make for a good relationship or marriage if two people have many differences in values and beliefs, unless they are willing to accept and respect each other's point of view.

70 Do you think that people should go steady at ages fifteen and sixteen?

At this age, it is probably better to date different people, so that you can find out what different people are like to be with. But often it doesn't work out that way. Sometimes, people feel pressured to become a steady couple. After they go out a few times, all their friends assume they are going steady. The boy and girl themselves also start to think of themselves as going steady. If either person dates another, everyone thinks he or she is "cheating." Often you may feel that you must either go steady or not date at all.

Going steady can provide a sense of security and a feeling that you are not alone. But it can also cut off chances to meet other interesting people. There are also other problems with steady dating. You may get bored with the other person, but it's hard to break up. To some people, going steady may mean the right to have sex. Putting off going steady may eliminate a lot of pressures.

71 When is the best age to get married?

There is no one answer appropriate to everyone. Any time between the ages of eighteen and thirty years or even older is common. Sometimes when a couple marry too early, they find that after a few years they have both changed and no longer have the same interests they did when they first married. People who have lived independently for a time usually have better marriages later on. People who go from their parents' home directly into a marriage often feel that they have missed a lot of significant life experiences, especially that of being on one's own.

Many people in this country do not get married until their late twenties or early thirties. This gives them a chance to graduate from college or get a more advanced degree, so they can get a better job. It also gives them a chance to travel, establish themselves in their careers, save up money to buy a house or car or just to "find" themselves before they enter into a long-term commitment.

Sometimes a couple get married early because the woman has become pregnant. It is better to avoid becoming pregnant accidentally. If you are in this situation, you need to talk to trusted adults about your options. If your parents aren't available, an adult you especially trust and respect — one you feel you can talk to confidentially — may be able to help you.

72 At what age is it best to have children?

Again, this is a difficult question to answer. Usually, it is best not to have a child as soon as you are married. It takes time to get to know the other person. At first you may be so sexually attracted to your partner that you don't notice much else about him or her. After awhile, you find that your partner has a terrible temper, or you can't stand the way he or she manages money. You may discover that, as you get to know your partner better and better, you love her or him more and more.

After a year or so, you will have a better idea of whether the marriage is going to last. Waiting awhile also gives you a chance to do things together that you can't do when you have young children to take care of. Waiting also gives you time to save up some money to pay for clothing, medical care and child care for your children.

73 Should you reach a certain age before you have intercourse? If so, what is that age? Should teenagers have sex?

There is no number that I can give you. Obviously, most 14-year-olds are much too young, and most 25-year-olds are more than old enough. It's a question of responsibility—you should only have intercourse if you are willing and able to accept the responsibilities involved and have the maturity to handle the emotions involved. Television and movies make intercourse look like a purely fun thing to do with no strings attached. They give you the impression that all you need to enjoy sex is the right kind of car or the right brand of jeans. In reality, sex is very enjoyable, but if you don't want it to be a devastating experience, you need to do some hard thinking and ask yourself some hard questions.

Most important is the question, "What will you do if you become pregnant or contract a sexually transmitted disease?" If you are firmly opposed to abortion under all circumstances, are you ready to take on the responsibility of raising a child for the next eighteen to twenty years? For the next five years, you need to be available for your child twenty-four hours a day, seven days a week, fifty-two weeks a year. Even if you think you are ready for the responsibility of raising a child, you simply may not be able to. Where are you going to earn enough money to house, feed and clothe him or her? Do you have a large sum of money saved for the medical expenses? Are you ready to quit school?

You should think about this question not only if you are a young woman, but also if you are a young man. A father is usually required to contribute to the support of his child until the child is eighteen years old. Aside from the economic question, each child needs a father as well as a mother to bring him or her up. Are you sure you are willing to stick around and help take care of the child, as well as contribute money to support it? Can your partner trust you to help her, day in and day out, for the next eighteen years? Whether you are a man or a woman, are you ready to postpone all career and educational plans for a long time so that you can earn money and provide care for your child?

If you think abortion is OK, how will it affect you to have one or to know that your girlfriend is having one because of you? You may think you would just shrug it off now, but try to think a little about how you would really feel. Do you know where to obtain one? How would your parents react? Does the law in your state require that they be told?

Second, do you know if your partner has a sexually transmitted disease? Do you know what to do if you contract one? Would your partner stick around to be with you through the treatment process?

Third, are you emotionally mature enough to accept the pain of a possible break-up? Sometimes one partner, more often the boy than the girl, thinks he loves the other when he is only feeling the desire to have sexual intercourse. Once he (or she) has achieved that goal, he (or she) disappears. Sometimes, one partner will deliberately mislead the other. Are you reasonably sure that your partner really is committed to you? Usually, you learn through experience how to tell if someone is really interested in you or is just "handing you a line." Have you had enough experience in relationships with members of the opposite sex to tell?

Fourth, do you know about birth control? Are you sure that both you and your partner know how to use a reliable birth control method properly all of the time?

If you are not sure about the answers to all of these questions, you are not ready to have intercourse. Many teens who have experienced some of the problems of intercourse, such as sexually transmitted diseases, pregnancy and deeply hurt feelings, have said, "It just wasn't worth it. I wish I had waited."

74 Who enjoys sex more, the man or the woman?

There is simply no way to give you a definite answer to this question. Both the male and the female are built to enjoy the experience of intercourse. A man enjoys sex in his own way, a woman enjoys sex in her own way. Many women are capable of multiple sexual orgasms. But enjoyment often depends upon the relationship and the situation. Teenage girls often do not enjoy intercourse because there is too much tension in the situation. Teen boys perhaps enjoy it more because they do not think as much about the problems that could result. See answer to Question 77, below.

75 Why do boys and girls like having oral sex?

It is a very stimulating form of sexual activity. As in other situations where the sex organs are directly touched, they arouse very strong sexual feelings, especially the desire for intercourse. This strong possibility should be taken into account before you are involved in the situation. A girl cannot get pregnant from oral-genital sex alone, and so sometimes it can be a way of having sexual pleasure and reaching a climax without risking pregnancy. This is so only if the feelings aroused do not lead the couple to engage in unprotected intercourse.

You should also know that you can easily catch a sexually transmitted disease (STD) from this activity (see the next question and the chapter on sexually transmitted diseases).

76 Is oral sex common? Do you think it is OK to do it?

Many kinds of sexual activity have been commonly practiced since the days that human beings lived in caves. Let me give you my way of telling whether a given kind of sexual activity is OK:

> Anything is all right in the area of sex as long as it doesn't hurt you and it doesn't hurt the other person, and as long as it doesn't offend you and it doesn't offend the other person.

People are different in what they enjoy. The feelings of the other person are just as important as your own feelings. Sex is part of a larger relationship. For example, suppose you are a girl and you are upset by the idea of putting your mouth on your boyfriend's penis, or of swallowing the discharge when he has a climax. If you feel this way, you have a right to say no, and should not give in to pressure to do something that does not feel enjoyable to you. Your own feelings are an important guide that you should listen to.

If you are a boy, you should not pressure your girlfriend to do something that she may find upsetting. The same is true for other forms of oral sex. Many people do not find this activity repugnant; it is important to overcome your shyness about discussing this issue with your partner. Above all, be clear in your own mind and tell your partner that you will take no for an answer. Even if you are "successful" at pressuring your partner into doing something she or he does not like, your partner may react to the unpleasant experience by losing his or her feelings for you.

77 I don't enjoy sex. Is there something wrong with me?

Many teenage girls do not enjoy sexual intercourse, although they may enjoy the closeness and the kissing, hugging and caressing. For some young women, intercourse can actually feel uncomfortable. Others may have almost no feeling at all. Often a woman does not enjoy sex because her body is very tense. This tension is the result of her discomfort with the sexual situation. Even a married woman may take a year or more to begin to enjoy intercourse, even though her husband enjoys it right from the start. This is because she has carried the tension and fear of pregnancy with her for so long that it takes a while for her to lose them.

Four very common sources of sexual tension and discomfort for women are:

1. Lack of privacy. A woman is much more comfortable having sex in her own home, rather than in the back seat of a car or in someone else's borrowed apartment.
2. Fear of pregnancy. A woman needs to be using a reliable method of contraception that she is confident that she and her partner know how to use (unless she wants to get pregnant).
3. Lack of tenderness from her partner. Most women want their partner to listen to their feelings, to respect their wishes and not to keep pressuring them to do things they do not want to do.
4. Lack of an ongoing relationship with someone she trusts. Many women only enjoy sex with someone they know will stay with them through whatever problems may develop in their relationship. Often, they may only feel comfortable about sex within marriage.

A lack of one or more of these conditions may easily make the woman anxious and produce tension in her body. Both anxiety and tension usually quickly cancel out pleasurable sexual feelings. Afterward, the woman may feel fear, anger, guilt or disappointment. If you are not enjoying sexual activity, try asking yourself if you are uncomfortable or feel guilty about what you are doing instead of simply blaming yourself.

Boys may also have less pleasure than they expect from sex. If you are a boy, perhaps you are having intercourse more to impress your friends than because you really want to. Perhaps you feel a little let down afterward because you are having sex with someone you don't especially care for. Or perhaps you do care for your partner and feel guilty for pressuring her to do something she doesn't really want to do.

78 I never have orgasms. Why is that?

Many teenage girls do not experience orgasm during intercourse. There is just too much tension in the whole situation. There is nothing wrong with the girl; the problem is that there is something wrong in the situation. See the answer to Question 77, above.[7]

79 When is sex the most enjoyable?

The enjoyment of sex is something that depends a great deal upon your maturity and how good your relationship is with your partner. For a teenager, sex may seem enjoyable because it is new and exciting. It seems like a daring and risky adventure into the hidden adult world. But sex that is experienced just for "kicks" soon becomes boring.

Boredom with sex may be the least of your problems if you contract a sexually transmitted disease, become pregnant or get your girlfriend pregnant. Fear of these two dangers often cancels out any enjoyment that the teenager might otherwise experience during intercourse. Unfortunately, this fear is very real. Rushing into intercourse could lead you to run into these problems head on, when you are not experienced enough to handle them.

Sex is usually enjoyed most when it takes place in a long lasting relationship, one in which each person expresses love and concern for the other and each person feels responsible for the happiness and health of the other. These conditions are most often found within marriage. In marriage, the couple is much more likely to relax and enjoy sex without the tensions and fears that unmarried people experience. Remember, many couples are married for twenty, thirty or forty years. You can look forward to enjoying sexual intercourse for all that time.

I would hope that you would not consider having intercourse until you are at least eighteen years old. At that time, you may be mature enough to take the long view of your life and decide if you wish to take the risks of intercourse. Don't misunderstand me; I am not saying that at age eighteen all the problems and responsibilities involved in sex will just disappear in a puff of smoke. Even then, you should make the decision deliberately and with much thought about your own future plans. Making this decision carefully will help you stay in control of your own life, and help you avoid having responsibilities and difficulties that you don't want to deal with yet.

80 I would like to have sex a lot more, but I'm afraid to.

Feeling scared of having intercourse is the beginning of good judgment for a teenager. Feelings by themselves are usually not a good guide to action by themselves, but they are important pointers that you need to do some thinking about a problem. Being scared of having intercourse shows that you are beginning to grow up and to think about the results of your actions. This is something that many teenagers don't do. Instead, they foolishly believe that they can have intercourse and nothing bad will happen to them because of it. They believe that they are leading a charmed life where everything ends happily ever after. Pregnancy or sexually transmitted disease, they think, just can't happen. They still believe that someone will take care of everything for them, just as their parents did when they were children. They are living in a fantasy world.

As you grow up, your thinking changes from that of a child to that of an adult. Children want what they want when they want it, with little thought for the future. If they want ice cream, they do not think about getting a stomach ache, gaining weight or having tooth cavities. Adults also want many things, but they usually have the mature judgment to decide what is good and right for them and what is not. Adults may decide to put off having something they want until they are ready to handle the consequences. Adults recognize their own limitations, and that having one thing often means giving up another—for example, getting a college degree means postponing having a child.

There is nothing wrong with wanting to have sex. But if you are an adult, before you act you will think about it and talk it over with adults you can trust. You might try your local family planning clinic. The counsellors there see teens every day who are struggling with this problem.

You also should talk it over with your boyfriend or girlfriend. If you can't talk frankly with your partner, you should ask yourself seriously whether you are in a good relationship or not.

REFERENCES

1. Bell, R. *Changing Bodies, Changing Lives.* New York: Random House, 1980, p. 131.
2. Kelly, G. F. *Learning About Sex.* New York: Barron's Educational Series, 1976, pp. 56–59.
3. Ibid. (Bell) pp. 79–81.
4. Ibid. (Kelly) pp. 31–32, 41–44.
5. Ibid. (Kelly) pp. 70–71.

6. Ibid. (Kelly) pp. 110–114.
7. Boston Women's Health Book Collective. *Our Bodies Ourselves.* New York: Simon and Schuster, 1976. pp. 44, 57–58.

Chapter IV

BIRTH CONTROL

1 What is birth control or contraception?

Birth control or contraception is the prevention of pregnancy. Its basic purpose is to allow a man and woman to enjoy sexual pleasure and sexual intercourse with each other, without having a pregnancy result.

It is practiced for many reasons. Often a couple wants to save up some money or establish themselves in their careers before they have their first child. Although they love each other and want to express their love sexually, they are not yet ready to have children. Or, they may have already had one or more children and have decided not to have any more. They may also use contraception to space their children apart, rather than having them one right after the other. Some couples decide they do not want to have children at all.

2 What are the chances for a woman of getting pregnant if she and her partner don't use any birth control method?

The chances are very high, especially for a teenager. A girl who has intercourse once per week will almost certainly become pregnant within six months. Even if it takes six months, she has had intercourse only twenty-six times. It has been found that a woman not past menopause who has regular intercourse has a ninety percent chance of becoming pregnant, unless she and her partner take steps to prevent pregnancy. If you think a couple you know has been having intercourse but the woman has not become pregnant, either they are using a birth control method, the woman ovulates (produces ripe eggs) very rarely, or you are mistaken! (Many teenagers, especially men, like people to think they are having intercourse when they are not.)

3 Is it a good method of birth control for the man to withdraw his penis from the woman's vagina just before he "comes" (ejaculates semen)?

No, this method is very unreliable. First of all, some semen, containing sperm, will have already come out of his penis inside the woman's vagina before he has ejaculated or "come." Although this is only a small amount of fluid, it only takes one sperm to make a woman pregnant. In fact, even

125

if his penis is right outside her vagina, a small amount of semen from his penis can leave sperm which may then find their way into the vagina.

Second, at the moment before a man is ready to come, the sexual pleasure is so intense that he has a very strong desire **not** to withdraw. The man may tell himself "just a few more seconds"—until it is too late.

4 If a woman washes her vagina or uses a douche, can that prevent her from becoming pregnant? Can taking a bath work?

Douching—washing the inside of the vagina—may sometimes work, but this is a very unreliable method of preventing pregnancy (or disease). During intercourse, the sperm are deposited in the cervix, which is the opening of the uterus. During ejaculation, the sperm quickly enter the uterus through the cervix. The cervix does not admit water or other fluids (such as those used in douches), so once inside the uterus, the sperm cannot be reached by washing or douching. If you think this method has worked once or twice for you or your girl friend, consider yourself very lucky; the chances are it won't work a third time.

Taking a bath has no chance of working, as the sperm are well inside the vagina where an ordinary bath won't reach them.

5 Are there certain times a woman is less likely to become pregnant? Is it true that if you have sex two weeks after the woman's period, your chances of getting pregnant are less?

Yes there are certain times that a woman with **very** regular menstrual cycles is more likely to become pregnant. However, two weeks after the woman's period is the **worst** time to have intercourse, because then she is most fertile (able to become pregnant). It is also very difficult for a teenage woman to know when sex is safe for her, because her cycles may not be regular for several years after she begins having periods.

Ovulation, the release of a ripe egg by an ovary, happens about half way between a woman's periods—two weeks before her next period begins if her cycle takes 28 days. Since sperm can live inside a woman for up to three days, if a woman has intercourse about three days before ovulation, she may become pregnant. She may also become pregnant if intercourse takes place within forty-eight hours after she ovulates.

Even a mature woman with a regular menstrual cycle cannot always determine when ovulation has occurred; to have a good idea, the woman must take her temperature every day and look for slight variations. Few women are so regular that they ovulate exactly the same number of days after their periods every month. For a teenager, it is almost impossible to determine reliably when ovulation has occurred, because her menstrual cycle is often still very erratic.[1]

6 Is it possible to miss a period and still not be pregnant?

Yes it is; in fact, missed periods are very frequent in young girls. For more on menstruation and pregnancy, see the chapter on Pregnancy and Childbirth.

7 Can you get pregnant during your period?

Yes, for some women it is possible to become pregnant at this time, although it is rare. A teenage woman whose cycle is not yet regular, may ovulate during her period, or mistake "spotting" for a period. For more on menstruation and pregnancy, see the chapter on Pregnancy and Childbirth.

8 How do you "do it" and not cause a pregnancy?

There is no one hundred percent sure way of having sexual intercourse and not having a pregnancy result, unless the woman has had her uterus removed surgically, her fallopian tubes tied or the man has had a vasectomy. There are several methods however with varying degrees of reliability; these will be discussed below.

To use any form of birth control requires two things: responsibility and communication. Don't assume that your partner will take care of contraception—both partners must share this responsibility. Many teenagers, especially young teenagers, do not take the trouble to learn how to use birth control methods correctly. Many don't use them at all. You also need to be honest with yourself and your partner about wanting to have sex and planning for it—something that is often very hard to do.

Sexual feelings often interfere with a teenager's judgment. When two people are alone together and strongly attracted to each other—the time when they should be using a birth control method—that may be the last thing on their minds. Often, this is because they have not admitted to themselves or to each other that they want to have sex, and so have not planned ahead. In the heat of the moment they have unprotected sex, and this is hardly the best time for them to figure out how to use any method that may be available.

If you are not mature enough to prepare in advance, if you are too embarrassed to discuss sexual intercourse with your partner ahead of time, if you don't trust yourself or your partner to make sure you use a birth control method carefully and properly when you are caught up in strong sexual emotions, then you probably should not have intercourse. Only if you have informed yourself about preventing pregnancy, and are sure you and your partner know how to use the method you have chosen, should you consider having intercourse. (Even more important in having intercourse is the ability to handle the strong emotions involved. See the Chapter on Sexual Expression and Sexual Relationships.)

9 Where can I obtain reliable birth control information and learn how to properly use birth control methods?

It is important to be well informed about birth control. This means that you must speak to health professionals: doctors, nurses, family planning clinic or women's health care center representatives or druggists. The best places are family planning clinics, women's health care centers or your doctor. You may go to a family planning clinic or women's health care center with your sexual partner. The trained counsellors there will explain to you exactly how to use the various methods, and will help you decide which is the best method for you. They also have physicians who can fit a woman with a diaphragm (discussed below) or write a prescription for birth control pills.

Don't rely upon your friends for advice. They probably know less than you do, although they may act like they know more. A young woman should not trust a man she doesn't know very well for advice on the safety and use of birth control methods—especially if the man is pressuring her to have sex with him. She needs to get the correct information from a less biased person.

10 How do I find out about the family planning services or women's health care centers in my neighborhood?

You can look under your county government or state government listings for family planning clinic, or call the general number for the state or county's offices. You can look up Planned Parenthood in the white business pages of the telephone book; you can also check listings under "women" for listing's like "women's health center," or "women's wellness center" in these same pages. You can also call a local hospital and ask for advice.

Your school's counselor may know of services available in your area, or ask a good friend where he or she goes for family planning. Don't rule out your parents completely! Mom or dad may surprise you with the information and support your needs.

11 How old do you have to be before you can buy condoms?

Many states are considering or passing laws regulating the sale of condoms. The best place to find out about this would be the local family planning agency. Presently, parents are not notified and a twelve-year-old may receive information and services at many family planning agencies. Druggists are allowed to sell non-prescription methods to teenagers, but many will not do so. They have this right. Many druggists feel that teens do not know how to use condoms properly or will use them incorrectly and get involved in venereal disease or pregnancy. A large store that has a pharmacy or health section will probably have condoms available. Your local Planned Parenthood office or health department may provide you with condoms at no charge.

12 How old must you be to obtain birth control methods like the pill and the diaphragm that require a doctor's prescription?

You can obtain these birth control devices from most family planning clinics or women's health care center any time after you are twelve years old. Before giving you condoms, they may require you to attend a class or two on how to use them properly. Don't be insulted—you're better off learning from experts. Prescription methods usually require the woman to have a physical examination.

The people there believe that if you are going to have sex, it is better for you to use a method to prevent pregnancy than to risk a pregnancy at an early age.

13 I don't have the money to buy prescription birth control devices or even condoms. How can I obtain them for free?

Many family planning clinics and women's health care centers will dispense them without charge. Often, they charge for services according to your ability to pay. If you can afford to pay a small fee, that is what they will charge; if you can't they may provide medical services and contraceptives free of charge.

14 How can I obtain birth control devices without my parents finding out?

Nonprescription methods may usually be found in the drug store or super market. They will not ask you for your name. Some druggists may or may not sell to teenagers. Family planning clinics and women's health care centers will supply them, often free of charge. They will also teach you how to use them properly. Condoms are also available in vending machines, but there is a risk that these condoms are low in quality or have been in the vending machine too long and have dried out, making them easy to break.

If you want the pill or the diaphragm, you may obtain these from a family planning clinic or women's health care center. In almost all places they will not inform your parents or anyone else—just to be sure, you may call the clinic on the telephone in advance to find out its policy. You may also go to a doctor of your own choosing. If you want to be sure you may ask the doctor what his or her policy is concerning informing your parents.

15 What is the most reliable method of birth control?

The most reliable method is this: not having intercourse. It works every time. For those who have decided that they are mature enough to practice birth control properly, there are several methods that are relatively reliable—although none is as reliable as abstinence.

So far the most reliable method is the birth control pill. Next comes the diaphragm. After that comes the condom used with contraceptive foam or the sponge. Finally, the least reliable is the condom used alone.

Due to recent litigation involving the use of IUDs (or intra-uterine devices), most companies manufacturing these devices have suspended production and/or sale of these products. Currently, very few physicians are willing to prescribe or insert an IUD. The physicians that continue to prescribe IUDs do so under very strict guidelines. The woman must meet these specific criteria:

1) she must be certain that she wants no children;
2) she must be in a monogamous relationship;
3) she must have no history of sexually transmitted infections.

There are other non-prescription methods available. Contraceptive suppositories are also available without a prescription at most drug stores. These are small, firm, bullet-shaped tablets that are inserted deep into the vagina before intercourse. They melt quickly and release nonoxynol-9 which kills sperm on contact, and provides some disease protection (Semicid).

The contraceptive sponge is another method. It is a small round piece of sponge-like material containing nonoxynol-9 and is inserted into the vagina to fit against the cervix and prevent sperm from traveling into the uterus and up into the fallopian tubes. It is inserted before intercourse and may be left in place up to twenty-four hours. Both the wearer and partner are unaware of its presence. It is a portable, hygienic and easily disposable method of birth control, although you may have some trouble when you first try to insert it. Its reliability is 85 to 90 percent effective, and that number is higher if used with a condom.

We shall discuss each available birth control method separately under the appropriate heading. The choice of the proper birth control method for you is a very important issue. It is best for you and your sex partner to discuss this issue with the trained professionals at a family planning clinic or with your family doctor. The choice depends upon many factors—what is convenient for you, how reliably you remember to take medications, your general health, how often you engage in sexual intercourse on the spur of the moment, how many partners you have.

For example, if you are forgetful about taking other medicines, then you will probably also forget to take the contraceptive pill some of the time, and this is probably not a good method for you.

On the other hand, if you often engage in sexual intercourse without thinking about it ahead of time, the diaphragm might not be for you, because you need to have thought ahead to bring it with you.

If you don't like mechanical devices or appliances, then the diaphragm is not for you—there's no point in using one if you sometimes put it in upside down.

If you have more than one sexual partner or frequently change partners, the condom with foam is a **must** for you. This method is thought to help prevent catching a sexually transmitted disease like AIDS or gonorrhea. In fact you can use a condom with foam together with another method like the diaphragm or the pill; that way you have the greater reliability that the diaphragm and pill give, and you also have the protection from disease that the condom with foam provides. Even if you don't like mechanical devices, it is very easy to learn to use a condom properly.[2]

16 For men, what are the available birth control devices?

A man who is not ready to give up ever having children has only three choices: the condom, the condom with contraceptive foam, and abstinence. (Strictly speaking foam is not a male contraceptive, because the foam is placed inside the woman's vagina just before intercourse, not on or around the man's penis.)

A man who is certain he does not want to father any more children can have a vasectomy. This operation is discussed below.

17 What is a "rubber" or condom for?

"Rubber" is a slang term for condom. A condom is a long, slender bag made out of latex or animal skin (usually lamb skin) that is slipped onto a man's erect penis. When the man has intercourse with a woman and is wearing a condom, the condom catches the man's sperm and prevents it from entering the woman's body. In this way it prevents her from becoming pregnant.

Condoms also sharply reduce the chances of contracting most venereal or sexually transmitted diseases, including AIDS, although they are not 100 percent safe. However, the latex condoms work much better than those of animal skin, because animal skin has pores that may let some germs through, including the AIDS virus. You should also check to see if they are lubricated or contain the spermicide **nonoxynol-9**. (If you prefer unlubricated condoms, use a foam or jelly that contains this chemical.) Because they prevent disease condoms are often used even when another method is also being employed.

18 How do you use a condom?

The best way to learn how to use a condom, or any other form of birth control, is to receive instruction at a family planning clinic or women's health care center. There are many possible mistakes that can be made. For example, it can be put on inside out, it can fall off, it can be broken, or semen can leak out of it into or near the woman's vagina. Your friends who tell you there's "nothing to it" probably don't know all the things that can go wrong, unless they have learned from a health professional.

The condom usually comes rolled up in a package so that it may be unrolled downward from the tip of the penis. There is also a small sack at the end of the bag to catch the semen. To put it on, squeeze the air out of this sack—leaving air in the sack often causes the condom to break, causing a high risk of pregnancy (and disease if one partner is infected with a sexually transmitted disease). Place the condom over the tip of the penis **when it is erect.** Then unroll it down the length of the penis. Don't start to put it on one way and then turn it around; this may carry semen from the penis to the outside of the condom, where it can then be left in the vagina.

If the condom isn't lubricated, you may prefer to use a lubricating product such as K–Y® Jelly or Surgi-Lube®. For added protection against pregnancy and disease, contraceptive foam or jelly containing nonoxynol-9 may be used as a lubricant. **Do not use** Vaseline®, hand lotions or other oil-based products. These will cause the condom to break and are very unhealthy for the vagina.

Before you start having intercourse is the time to put the condom on; once you start, a small amount of semen can leave sperm in the woman's vagina even though the man has not ejaculated.

After intercourse, as the penis is withdrawn, the condom should always be held onto the penis, to prevent any spillage. You need to obtain good quality condoms and to become familiar with how to use them properly. It's not a good idea to carry one around in your wallet for a long time; it is likely to become dried out and break easily. The condom is much more reliable when used with contraceptive foam or jelly. The condom may only be used once and should be discarded after use.

Condoms may be easily purchased in a drug store without a prescription, and may be obtained free of charge at many family planning clinics.

19 How reliable is the condom?

Condoms work well if used properly. But there is always a real chance that it will break, that there will be a small hole in it, that it will come off during intercourse or that semen will spill during intercourse or after withdrawal. The condom by itself works 90 to 98 percent of the time; this means that of 100 couples using the condom, 2 to 10 will risk a pregnancy. The use of foam with the condom further decreases the chances of pregnancy.[3]

20 What happens if the condom comes off during intercourse?

The woman may become pregnant. This is a common problem, but it can usually be avoided if either of the partners hold the condom on at the base of the penis after you are finished having intercourse, as the man is withdrawing. This is also a good reason to use contraceptive foam. The foam kills sperm and most disease organisms, even if some semen enters the vagina. It provides double protection.

21 Are condoms effective against all forms of venereal disease?

No, but they are effective against the more serious ones—although they are not 100 percent effective so there is always some risk. Latex condoms are much more effective than natural skin ones; condoms made of skin have pores that can allow tiny organisms, including the AIDS virus, to pass through. Condoms are not considered effective against herpes, genital warts or pubic lice (crabs).

22 Why can't you use a balloon, a plastic bag or plastic wrap instead of a condom? Suppose you use foam with it?

Balloons, plastic bags and plastic wrap are not reliable. If you use one with foam, only the foam will have any effect, and foam by itself is not very reliable.

23 What is foam?

Foam is a chemical that kills sperm. It comes in a small aerosol can and looks very much like shaving cream or hair mousse when it is released from the container. It has the chemical nonoxynol-9 in it to kill sperm, and acts as a barrier to prevent sperm from entering the cervix. Foam is dispensed from the can into a plastic applicator, which is then inserted into the vagina. Pressing the plunger on the applicator pushes the foam into the vagina. The applicator must be washed after each use, and should never be shared with anyone. Some brands of foam come in prefilled, one-use disposable applicators.

24 Is foam OK to use by itself?

No it is not. By itself contraceptive foam is not very reliable. But it makes such other methods as the condom and the diaphragm much more reliable (it is not necessary with the pill). A jelly-like product is also made that can be used instead of the foam. These products are available at any drugstore and most large supermarkets without a prescription. They are also available at family planning centers and women's health clinics.

25 How does the "pill" work? How reliable is it?

The oral contraceptive pill also prevents pregnancy, but it works in a very different way from the condom. It contains hormones that change a woman's egg-producing cycle so that she will not become pregnant. They stop her ovaries from releasing ripe eggs. Then, even if there is sperm present in her fallopian tubes, she cannot become pregnant. The pill doesn't kill the egg or the baby. In fact it doesn't kill anything. It just stops the body from releasing a ripe egg. It works **before** the egg and sperm ever have a chance to meet.

This method is the most reliable, so long as the woman remembers to take her pill each day (or according to the directions given in her prescription). When a woman decides she wants to become pregnant, she stops taking the pill, and soon her ability to become pregnant returns. But no method except surgical sterilization is completely reliable. Occasionally women who take the pill still become pregnant. We don't always know why. Other medicines, such as antibiotics, may prevent the pill from working properly. Sometimes the hormones don't act on their bodies the same as they do in those of most women. No method of birth control is 100 percent safe except abstinence or not having intercourse.

You need to know that the birth control pill **cannot** be used as you do medicines that you take "only when you need it," like aspirin. A woman cannot wait to take it only just before or just after she has sex. She must take it regularly according to her doctor's instructions, whether or not she expects to be having sex within the next week or two.

However, the pill does not protect either partner against sexually transmitted diseases. Unlike the condom, foam and the diaphragm, it does not create a barrier against the disease-causing germs.

26 How old should a woman be before she begins taking the pill?

It is usually best for a woman to wait until she is fully physically mature and has stopped growing (possibly about sixteen to eighteen years of age). When a woman is still growing, larger than usual amounts of hormones are present in her body, and it is better not to add still more hormones with birth control pills.

However, a woman who is frequently having sexual intercourse is better off using the pill, if the alternative is pregnancy; teen pregnancy will be much harder on her body than the pill.

27 Does the pill cause breast or other forms of cancer? What other diseases are associated with the pill? Does it have any beneficial effects?

All of the facts on this question are not yet in. It may have a slightly increased chance of causing breast and cervical cancer in some women. However, it is also known to **decrease** the chances of having cancer of the ovaries or uterus. The pill is also known to decrease the likelihood of ovarian cysts, some forms of arthritis, pelvic infections and other problems.

Birth control pills are also associated with a somewhat higher risk of blood clots, which can cause heart attacks, strokes and other problems. However, this risk is considered slight for women under age 30. Women over 35 who take the pill, especially if they also smoke, do have a much greater chance of dying from a heart attack or stroke.

There are several different kinds of pills available, with different kinds and different amounts of hormones in them. If one is not appropriate for you, another may be. You need to discuss your personal medical history and your family's medical history with the physician who may prescribe birth control pills for you. If you or your family have a history of stroke or heart problems, high blood pressure, breast or uterine cancer, you should bring this up with the doctor.

The pill may have side effects for some women—ask your doctor for a list of these. The side effects may include headaches, sleeplessness, nausea, weight gain and others.

28 What is the diaphragm?

The diaphragm is a flexible dome-shaped disk that is inserted into the woman's vagina so that it covers the opening to her uterus (the cervix). It is used with a contraceptive jelly or cream that kills sperm. That way, the sperm cannot enter the uterus to begin their journey to the fallopian tubes. Although some couples find it too mechanical and unromantic, others don't mind it and make inserting it a part of sexual foreplay. It is very reliable when properly used, and has the additional advantage that it does not involve long term taking of drugs that may have harmful side-effects for some women. It is a prescription method and comes in several sizes. The woman needs to be fitted for her correct size.

29 What is the IUD or intrauterine device?

The IUD is still another way of preventing pregnancy. There are several kinds. They are small objects that are inserted into a woman's uterus by a doctor. It is not known exactly how they work, but they do prevent pregnancy. They may only be inserted or removed by a physician, and may not be obtained in any other way. Some IUDs have caused injury to the uterus and sometimes infertility.

30 What is the rhythm method?

The rhythm method involves having intercourse at those times in the menstrual cycle when the woman's egg is not present. It requires that the woman have regular periods and that she and her partner keep track very accurately of where she is in her menstrual cycle.

The rhythm method is not very reliable. It is particularly unsuitable for teenage women, because their menstrual cycles are usually not well established yet and are very irregular. A woman may mistake "spotting" for her period, for example. She may also have eggs available to start babies more than once a month even though she only has one period per month.

31 Is abortion a good form of birth control?

No, abortion is a very bad form of birth control. We do not know all the reasons why women have abortions, but it is too serious because it involves surgery, although the operation is relatively easy and has few complications.

An abortion can be an emotionally painful experience for the woman, and often for the man responsible as well. It is also a surgical procedure, and **any** surgery should not be entered into lightly. While you may consider abortion a better option than having a child that you are unable or unwilling to love and provide for, it is no lark. For more on abortion, see the chapter on Pregnancy And Childbirth.

32 Are there operations that men and women can have that will make it certain that they can't have children?

Yes there are. A man may have a **vasectomy**. A woman may have a **tubal ligation**. These are virtually foolproof. However, these are almost never performed on teenagers. Only people who are certain that they will never want to have any more children under any circumstances have these operations, as they are very difficult to reverse. Reversals may be attempted, but the odds of success are less than fifty percent. A vasectomy is more difficult to reverse, especially if the original surgery was performed long ago. Both types of surgery should be considered permanent. Almost all the people who have these operations are older adults who have already had children or are mature enough to decide that they do not want to have any.

A **vasectomy** is a safe and simple operation that can be done in a doctor's office, under local anaesthetic, in about 20 minutes. The doctor disconnects the tubes called the **vas deferens.** Sperm can no longer travel from the testicles through the man's body to his penis, although he will still have semen.

A **tubal ligation** involves the clamping or sealing of both fallopian tubes. This prevents any eggs from reaching the uterus. It takes about an hour, is done under either local or general anaesthesia, and may require an over-night hospital stay. It involves two small incisions near the navel, through which instruments are inserted that clamp or cauterize the fallopian tubes.

Neither of these operations affects the person's sexual desire, as the organs which produce sex hormones are still in full operation.[4]

REFERENCES

1. Hatcher, Robert A.; Guest, F.; Stewart, F.; Stewart, G. K.; Trussel, James; Owen, Sylvia; Cates, Willard. *Contraceptive Technology.* New York: Irvington Publishers, 1988, pp. 355–357.
2. Ibid. (Hatcher) pp. 151.
3. Boston Women's Health Book Collective. *Our Bodies Ourselves.* New York: Simon and Schuster, 1976, pp. 203–205.
4. Ibid. (Hatcher) pp. 401–420.

Chapter V

SEXUALLY TRANSMITTED DISEASES

A. GENERAL QUESTIONS

1 What is "VD"? What is an "STD"?

"VD" stands for "venereal disease" and "STD" stands for "sexually transmitted disease." Both terms refer to the various diseases that one person may give to another through sexual activity—usually, but not always, through sexual intercourse. The word "venereal" derives from the Greek goddess of love, Venus. It has been known for many centuries that sexual intercourse may spread certain diseases. The term "venereal disease" is no longer used by health professionals to describe these diseases. Instead they use "sexually transmitted disease" or STD.

There are about twenty different STDs in the world. The ones of most concern in the United States are gonorrhea, syphilis, herpes, chlamidya, hepatitis and AIDS. All of these diseases are serious. Some can cause serious harm or even death. AIDS is virtually always fatal.

The organisms that carry these diseases thrive in the warm, moist membranes of the penis, vagina, rectum and throat; they are easily transmitted during sexual intercourse and oral sex. Many of them are also passed through contact with the blood of an infected person, such as when drug addicts share needles. Most cannot be transferred unless there is intimate bodily contact. Often babies of infected mothers are born with the disease.

2 How did venereal disease get started? Did humans first catch STDs by having sex with animals?

We really don't know how these diseases started. Like many other diseases, most venereal or sexual transmitted diseases have been around for thousands of years—before history began to be written down. They have been handed down from one generation to the next for all that time.

It is very doubtful that any form of STDs came from an animal, as the known animal STDs cannot be passed on to humans.

143

3 Can you get STDs or AIDS when you are a teenager, even if you are only in the 8th grade?

You certainly can. Even an infant can contract these diseases—usually because its mother had the disease before it was born. It is foolish to think that "it can't happen to me." Public health officials say that one in ten teenagers contacts an STD. Many of them don't even know they are ill. They don't go to a doctor until months or years after they have caught the disease, when it has had time to do serious damage which can never be corrected. Most of these diseases can be cured or at least kept under control, so it is important to go to a doctor or VD clinic immediately if you suspect you may have an STD.

4 If I only sleep with "nice" people, I don't have to worry about STDs, do I?

Yes, you do. A "nice" person can get an STD and give it to you as much as anyone else. Remember, when you have sex with someone, you are exposing yourself to all the diseases that person's other sexual partners are carrying, and all the diseases those partners' partners may have. If you have sex with someone who has slept with only five other people, and each of these people has had sex with five people, that adds another twenty-five people, for a total of thirty people who could be carrying an STD. And if each one of those additional twenty-five people slept with only five people . . . well, you get the idea.

5 If you have sex with several people at the same time, does this increase your chances of catching an STD?

Whether you have sex with several people in one evening or with several people on different evenings doesn't make any difference as to your chances of contracting an STD. What does increase your chances is having many sexual partners—the more you have, the more likely you are to catch a disease.

6 How do you catch an STD? Can you get an STD if you don't have sexual intercourse? What about oral sex?

Venereal diseases or STDs are usually transmitted through sexual intercourse. However, the organisms that cause them can grown in any warm, moist part of the body that air doesn't get to. This includes not only the penis and vagina, but also the rectum and the throat, but not the mouth which has air constantly circulating in it.

So you can catch most STDs through oral-genital sex—from a "blow job" or from "eating out" a woman. You can also catch them through anal intercourse. AIDS and some other STDs can be caught by drug addicts who share needles, as the organisms that cause the disease are in the bloodstream of an infected person, and small amounts of infected blood left on the needle may introduce the disease into someone else's blood.

Herpes is especially easy to catch. You can contract herpes by touching the blisters on another person and then touching some other moist part of your own body. AIDS, syphilis and gonorrhea are only caught by close sexual contact or the transfer of an infected person's blood into the bloodstream of another.

A baby may catch many of these diseases from its mother's blood, and when it travels down the birth canal at birth.[1]

7 Can you catch STDs from a virgin?

Obviously, a virgin—a person who has never had sexual intercourse—could have had oral sex or injected illegal drugs, and so caught one of these diseases.

8 Can you catch an STD by having anal sex?

You certainly can. The rectum, to which the anus leads, is a warm, moist place where air does not circulate—just the kind of place where many STD organisms will multiply and spread.

9 Can you catch an STD by being near someone who has one, or by hugging or kissing? Are door knobs, drinking cups or wet toilet seats safe? Can you catch it from animals?

You cannot catch an STD just by being in the same room with someone, as you can with a cold or the flu. You can't catch one by hugging or kissing, except for herpes, which you can catch if your mouth contacts herpes sores on another person's mouth, and possibly Hepatitis B. Less serious STDs like pubic lice (commonly referred to as "crabs") may also be caught without direct contact with an infested person, as they live on furniture and bed sheets. You cannot catch more serious STDs from a toilet seat, a glass, a door knob or by contact with animals. The organisms causing most STDs cannot live in light and air. For more extensive discussions of how each STD may be transmitted, see questions on the individual diseases, below.[2]

10 Which diseases are passed on by kissing?

One sexually transmitted disease that you can catch by kissing is herpes, and only if the other person has herpes blisters around his or her mouth.

Of course you can catch other diseases such as colds, the flu, even mononucleosis by kissing. The best way to prevent this is to make sure you eat and sleep properly, and get regular exercise—in short, by keeping yourself in good health.

11 Can you catch an STD through masturbation?

You can't catch an STD through masturbation alone. However, if you touch another person's sexual organs, you may become infected from that person, and visa versa. If you do have an STD, you need to avoid touching your genitals when the disease is producing sores or blisters on your sexual organs, so that you don't spread the disease to other parts of your body.

12 Does one sex pass on an STD more than the other?

STDs are passed on by both males and females.

13 Who is more likely to get an STD, a man or a woman?

Women are probably somewhat more susceptible to catching a sexually transmitted disease each time they have intercourse, because the man's infected semen is deposited inside her body.

14 Why do men often find out more quickly than women that they have an STD?

In men, the disease often produces symptoms that may be very noticeable right away. Gonorrhea, for example, produces an infection in the urethra, the tube which opens at the end of his penis. When a man urinates, the infection may produce a lot of pain. However, about one in five men with this infection do not have this type of pain. Syphilis usually produces a sore or chancre right on the penis.

In women, these same symptoms of infection often occur inside of the vagina where the woman can't see or feel them. They are less likely to be painful as well.

15 How can a person find out she or he has an STD if his or her partner doesn't tell her?

If a person doesn't have any symptoms, he or she can still be tested regularly at the county clinic—twice a year if sexually active with more than one partner, or if the person's partner is having sex with other people. The important thing is to not fall into the habit of thinking, "it can't happen to me." Someone who does not face the possibility of having an STD could wind up with permanent damage to his or her reproductive system or to other bodily organs.

16 How long after having sex will you first realize that you have an STD?

It depends greatly on the type of disease and on the individual involved. It may be as little as a few days after intercourse that the first symptoms show up, such as pain or burning during urination (a symptom of gonorrhea). Sores or chancres around the genitals (symptoms of syphilis) may show up two to three weeks after intercourse. These symptoms often disappear quickly, or you may not have any symptoms at all. It takes several years for AIDS symptoms to appear.

17 How can you tell if you have an STD? Why don't people know if they have an STD?

Six common symptoms include:

1) an unusual, pus-like or smelly discharge from the penis or vagina—it may be white, yellowish, greenish or clear in color;
2) pain or a burning sensation when you urinate (in both men and women);
3) a sore that looks serious but doesn't hurt very much around the private parts—sometimes about the size of a quarter—that goes away after about three weeks;
4) blisters of any size around or inside the sexual organs that are very painful;
5) a rash around the genital areas or elsewhere on the body
6) pain during or after intercourse, or, for a woman, very bad cramps about the time of her menstrual period.

Each disease has different symptoms, but you can have an STD with no symptoms at all—about a third of all people who catch an STD do not have any of these symptoms. It is very important to remember that the symptoms we have described often go away after a while, **but this does not** mean that the disease has gone, that it is less dangerous to your body or that you can no longer infect someone else.

18 If you have been having sex, but don't have any symptoms, do you need to worry?

Yes you do. Syphilis and gonorrhea are called the "great masqueraders" because they produce symptoms that resemble other less serious diseases. Moreover, the initial symptoms usually go away fairly quickly. The disease organisms may work their damage on a bodily organ for three months or more without attracting your attention. Only when they have damaged an organ enough to make you sick do you realize that there is a serious problem. AIDS is even more insidious because it usually produces no symptoms at all for several years.

Even if you have no symptoms, if you have been having sexual intercourse, particularly with several partners, or injecting yourself with illegal drugs, it is a good idea to be tested for STDs twice a year. You need to specifically ask your doctor to test you, as these tests are not usually routinely given as part of a general physical examination. But if you have never had intercourse, engaged in oral or anal sex or taken illegal drugs, you don't need to worry.

19 How can you tell if someone else has an STD?

You usually cannot tell. Even a doctor cannot always tell just by looking at or examining someone—often laboratory tests are necessary to be sure. But if you see that your sex partner has a sore, blisters or a rash on or near the genitals, blisters on the mouth or a rash on the skin, you should be concerned both for your own safety and your partner's health, and not have sex with that person until he or she has been given a clean bill of health by a doctor.[3]

20 Does an odor from the vagina or penis mean that a person has an STD? Does the odor mean that STD germs are spreading to me?

An odor from the man's penis is probably due to lack of bathing. If it persists despite good cleanliness, the man should consult a doctor. A vaginal odor does not usually mean the woman has STD. It is often a symptom of some other kind of vaginal infection, an infection that can cause long-lasting problems if it is not treated. A woman who has an odor that does not go away after she bathes should consult a doctor. We don't always know why a woman has an infection; it doesn't mean that she has been "sleeping around" or even that she has been having intercourse at all.

No STD is spread through the air or by a smell.

21 If a woman has an STD, will she still have her period?

Most probably she will. Severe cramps around the time of menstruation can be a symptom of an STD, but a woman may not realize that that is the problem, especially if she has had bad cramps before. Only when the cramps become extremely painful will she go to a doctor or hospital emergency room. This may mean that she has pelvic inflammatory disease (PID), which can infect her fallopian tubes. Such an infection can damage the tubes so that she may have difficulty getting pregnant, or be unable to conceive at all.

22 A creamy foam has been flowing out of my penis. Does this mean that I have an STD?

It may very well mean that you do, as it is a frequent symptom of several STDs. Even if the discharge goes away, you need to get checked immediately. Any condition in your body that is different needs to be checked out by a doctor or nurse-practitioner.

23 Does vaginal pain, especially during intercourse, mean I have an STD?

It could be a sign that you have herpes blisters inside the vagina, as these are very painful. It could also mean that you have some other problem, like an infection. Even if the pain goes away, this needs to be checked by a doctor or nurse-practitioner.

24 What do you do if you think you have an STD?

In almost every county of every state in this country, there is a free VD clinic. You should go there at once if you suspect you might have an STD. This is very hard to do, but you can trust the people at the clinic not to tell anyone about your visit and the subsequent results.

No one will find out you have been there unless you tell them. Often, when you are tested the clinic will give you a number. When you call back to find out the results of your tests, you will give your number. That way, if someone else called up pretending to be you, the clinic would not give out the information. Even if your parents call to ask if you have been there, clinic personnel will not tell them. You can ask the clinic personnel about this before you give your name, or even over the telephone.

You will be given tests by a doctor or nurse. If they find out that you have a sexually transmitted disease, they will not tell your parents although they are required by law to ask you for the names of the people you have had intercourse with, so that they can assist you in having these individuals tested and treated, so you can avoid being reinfected. The clinic will have them come in for treatment. All names are required to be sent to the state health department—but these are kept confidential and used to determine how many cases of STDs each county has.

If they find that you have gonorrhea or syphilis, they may give you antibiotic shots on the spot to begin treatment. If they are not sure whether you have a disease, they will ask you to call back after they have obtained the test results.

25 How do they test for STDS?

There are two kinds of tests, a blood test and a smear of fluid taken from the tip of the penis or the inside of the vagina. The blood test involves only a pin-prick, and the smear is completely painless.

If you have been having oral sex, you need to tell the medical personnel, as this requires a different test for an STD, involving swabbing for the fluid in your throat. They will probably ask you what kind of sexual activity you have engaged in.

It is important to get tested right away. With herpes, if you wait until the blisters go away, doctors may not be able to tell whether you have herpes until the blisters return.

26 Why do many people who have an STD not tell anyone?

People often feel uncomfortable talking about matters related to sex. When people have STDs, they can feel even more uncomfortable. Often they fear that people will think they have been having sex with the "wrong" kind of people or that they are too "easy." Or they may simply not want other people, like their parents, to find out that they have been having sex. But any infected person has an obligation to tell his or her sexual partner(s), because the partner may also have become infected with an STD.

27 Can a person have two or more STDs at the same time?

Yes, this is quite possible. The more partners you have, and the less you know about them, the more likely it is that you will catch an STD, two STDs or even more. This is one area in which you probably don't want to make it into the Guinnes Book of Records!

28 How do STDs affect your body?

Each disease affects the body and different people differently. Gonorrhea can damage the reproductive organs so that the person cannot have children. The disease-causing organisms can also travel to other organs and damage them. AIDS gradually destroys the immune system so that the person eventually dies from some other disease that the body can no longer defend itself against. For more specific information, see the discussion of the major diseases below.

29 Can STDs kill you?

Only AIDS is likely to kill you. While other diseases like syphilis and gonorrhea might eventually kill you, they will make you sick enough to go to a doctor a long time before you die. The doctor will be able to halt the disease. Babies are more likely to die from an STD than older people. In other parts of the world where most people do not have access to medical doctors, many people still die of these diseases. But even if you are cured of one of these diseases, doctors usually cannot undo the damage it has already done.

30 Can a woman with an STD still get pregnant?

Yes, she certainly can, and the baby can catch the disease from its mother.

31 If a woman with an STD becomes pregnant, will the STD harm her baby?

Yes. If she remains untreated her baby may be born not only infected, but severely damaged or even dead. The baby may also catch an STD during birth as it passes through the vagina. This is another reason for a woman to see a doctor as soon as she suspects she is pregnant. If syphilis is discovered within the first three months of pregnancy, it can be cured and will not damage the baby. Otherwise, the baby may be deformed or be born dead. Even herpes can injure or kill the baby. Although herpes cannot be cured, doctors can possibly prevent the baby from catching the virus during birth. They may do a Caesarean delivery so that the baby avoids the birth canal. If a girl has ever had a sore vagina, she needs to tell her doctor or midwife about it, so he or she can protect the baby from catching an STD during the birth process.

AIDS can also be passed to the baby from the mother's blood; if the mother has AIDS, there is a 50 percent chance that her child will be born with this fatal disease.

If a girl has ever had a sore vagina, she must tell her doctor about it, so he can protect the baby from catching any STDs during the birth process.

32 Can my baby be mentally retarded if I have an STD while I'm pregnant?

Yes it could. It could also be deformed. That is one reason why a woman should go to a doctor as soon after she becomes pregnant as possible. If you are diagnosed with a sexually transmitted disease, the doctor can usually treat you so that your baby will not be harmed.

33 Is there a cure for most STDs?

Some can be cured, like gonorrhea and syphilis. The doctor will prescribe penicillin or a similar drug if you are allergic to penicillin. The treatment takes about ten days, but is no protection against having the same or another STD a second or more times. If you have sexual contact again with someone who has the disease, you may become reinfected.

Herpes is not curable, but it may appear only once or only reoccur occasionally. It can cause a great deal of discomfort, but does not seem to cause serious harm. There are medications that can make the blisters less painful and speed healing for some people.

AIDS at present cannot be cured, although some progress is being made in keeping AIDS sufferers alive and functioning for longer and longer periods of time.

34 Will there ever be a cure for herpes or AIDS?

Probably there will be. A great deal of research is being devoted to understanding and curing these diseases. For AIDS, thousands of scientists are trying to conquer this disease, which is nearly always fatal. Scientists do not expect to find a cure or a vaccine for AIDS in the near future.

Scientists are somewhat more optimistic about developing a cure for herpes, or a vaccine that will immunize people against it, as they now have for polio and the measles. (A vaccine does not cure people who already have a disease, but it prevents them from catching it in the first place).

35 Do STDs ever go away by themselves?

Most do not. Your symptoms, the rash or burning, may go away, but the disease itself continues to silently progress inside your body, causing damage to important organs. It may be difficult to believe that you have a serious disease when you feel fine and have no symptoms. Don't fool yourself into believing you can ignore symptoms you had a few weeks or months ago. If you are regularly having sex with different partners, don't assume that you're safe even if you have never had any symptoms; get tested at least twice a year.

36 Will bathing, douching (washing the inside of the vagina) eliminate a sexually transmitted disease?

If you wash very soon after sex, it **may** prevent the disease organisms from spreading, but you can't count on this method to work. Douching is not very effective—the germ lives in the cells of the mucus membrane and cannot be washed out.[4]

37 How can you avoid catching an STD? Is a condom reliable?

The best way to avoid catching an STD is to know your sexual partner well. You should know whether she or he has had many sexual partners. You should not have sex with someone who is "sleeping around," and you should avoid having many brief sexual relationships yourself.

You should not have sex with anyone who injects illegal drugs with a needle, and you should not take such drugs yourself. Before marriage, couples usually have themselves tested for STDs; if they are both free of disease, they need not worry so long as they only have sex with each other. If you think you are "getting serious" with someone and you want to have sex, you and your partner could both be tested so that you don't have to worry.

A condom made of **latex** is also a good way to prevent most STDs. However condoms are not fool-proof, and condoms have not been shown to prevent herpes. You need to use one **every** time you have sex. Sheep-

or lamb-skin condoms are not safe because the skins have tiny pores that can allow some disease organisms, including the AIDS virus, to get through.

Using a foam containing **nonoxynol-9** with a condom greatly decreases your chances of catching an STD, because the chemical nonoxynol-9 kills many disease organisms, including the AIDS virus. However, **you should avoid using vaseline, hand lotion, massage oil, or other oil-based lubricants with a condom,** as these may break it and are not healthy for the vagina.

Unless you are sure that you and your partner are having sex only with each other and that neither of you has already contracted an STD, you should always insist on the use of a condom. You should not have sex with anyone who refuses to use a condom. Someone who refuses simply does not care enough about you or your health. You should not trust or be intimate with this individual.

B. ACQUIRED IMMUNE DEFICIENCY SYNDROME (AIDS)

38 What is AIDS?

AIDS stands for "acquired immune deficiency syndrome." It is a disease that attacks the immune system, the system that prevents the millions of organisms, the viruses and bacteria all around us from seriously damaging our bodies. When they start to infect us, the immune system's white blood cells detect the disease-causing organisms and destroy them, either before they create an infection or after they begin one. When you have a cold or the flu, most of the symptoms are caused by the body gearing up its defenses to fight off an invading organism.

The AIDS virus takes over certain of the immune system's white blood cells (called T-4 helper cells) so that they no longer fight off infections. It may take many years for this infection to damage the immune system enough for symptoms to appear—as much as ten or more years. Although some medicines have been discovered to slow the advance of the disease, there is no known cure. It is expected that virtually everyone who contracts AIDS will eventually die from it unless new treatments and/or cures are discovered.

39 If you test positive for the HIV-virus, does this mean that you have AIDS?

No. A positive test means that you have the HIV-virus in your blood-stream and body, and that you can give it to other people. This is the virus which causes AIDS. You may eventually develop AIDS, but we do not know whether everyone infected with the virus develops the disease.

40 Where did AIDS come from?

Unlike other STDs, AIDS is a disease that seems to have appeared only within the last fifteen or twenty years. It is believed to have originated in Africa, where a certain type of monkey is known to carry a virus very similar to the AIDS virus.

41 How can you tell if another person is HIV-positive or has AIDS?

You can't tell unless the person lets you know. As with other STDs, only medical tests can determine whether an individual is HIV-positive or has AIDS.

42 If another person looks healthy and feels OK, can I still get AIDS from him or her?

Yes you can. It often takes many years after infection with the AIDS virus for symptoms to appear, but AIDS can be transmitted to another person—like you—shortly after it enters the other person's body.[5]

43 How do you catch AIDS? Will you get AIDS if you don't have sex? Will you catch it from hugging or kissing?

AIDS is caught through sexual contact, usually sexual intercourse. The virus is present in the man's semen, the fluids of the woman's vagina and the rectums of people who already have the disease, so you may catch it by having intercourse with an infected person.

However, you can also catch AIDS without having sex. If you take intravenous drugs, you may catch it by sharing needles with others. This is because the AIDS virus is present in the blood of people who are already infected. Many drug addicts are now infected.

AIDS is a dose-specific disease—that means, a specific amount of the AIDS virus must be present for someone to "catch" the disease. That's why you cannot catch the AIDS virus by simple things like hugging, shaking hands or dry-kissing an AIDS victim or someone who is carrying the virus. Nor can you catch it from being in a room where an AIDS sufferer has sneezed. You can't get it by eating the same food or by sharing a glass or drinking fountain with an infected person. You can't get it from a toilet seat. A mosquito that bites an AIDS patient and then bites you will not give you the disease. Members of families with children with AIDS who bathe or hug their children every day do not contract AIDS.

You cannot catch AIDS by donating blood. If you **receive** donated blood during a surgical operation or because of a loss of blood, there is a very small chance you may contract AIDS, even though all blood donated since the end of 1985 has been tested for AIDS.

44 Can a woman with AIDS have a healthy baby?

It is very risky for a woman with AIDS to have a baby. There is a fifty percent chance that the baby will contract AIDS while it is inside the mother. It may also be passed to the child through breast milk. Most of these children die before the age of three years.

45 How can you tell if you have AIDS?

There is a test for AIDS that will determine if the virus is present in a person's body. However, it does not give reliable results until several months after the person has become infected. This test cannot tell when or whether the person will actually become ill, and scientists disagree on whether all people who carry the virus will eventually develop AIDS.

The following symptoms could be signs of AIDS and should be checked out with a doctor or at a clinic: swollen glands in the neck, underarm or groin areas; white spots, usually in the mouth; fever; night sweats; weight loss; persistent diarrhea; a constant tired feeling; flu-like symptoms; vaginal infections; fatigue; black and blue spots, or a combination of some or all of the above symptoms. Remember: any of these signs may take months or even years to appear.

46 How can you prevent catching AIDS?

Unprotected vaginal or anal intercourse, or oral sex, are extremely risky if you don't know the sexual history of your partner. As with other STDs, staying with one partner, and having a partner who is not having sex with others is good protection.

However, many teenagers experience a number of sexual relationships before they find a long-term partner. For this reason you should always use a latex condom with spermicidal foam or jelly. Make sure the foam or jelly contains **nonoxynol-9**, as this chemical kills the AIDS virus. **Lamb or sheep-skin condoms are to be avoided,** as they may allow the AIDS virus to pass through them.

Drug addicts who cannot give up their habits can avoid catching the disease either by not sharing needles, or by flushing the needle with a mixture of one part Clorox bleach to ten parts water before they use it.

47 Should I be tested for the AIDS virus?

If you have had unprotected sex with one or more sex partners you should be tested. If you have been engaging in risky activity—especially unprotected homosexual intercourse or oral sex—you should be tested. If you take illegal intravenous drugs you should be tested. If you have a partner who has done any of these things, you should be tested. If you had a blood transfusion before 1986 you should be tested.

However, before you are tested you should seek counselling, as a positive test can have a severe emotional impact, and in some situations may do more harm than good. There is much debate as to whether early detection of infection can allow doctors to prevent or delay the appearance and course of the disease.

48 If I am tested, will other people find out about it?

Some governmental agencies cannot guarantee confidentiality. But other testing agencies provide absolute secrecy by not taking your name, and simply assigning you a number. You give the number when the test results come back. You can ask before you are tested—perhaps over the telephone. Protecting your confidentiality is very important, as some insurers will not insure someone who tests positive, and many employers discriminate against carriers of the AIDS virus.

C. OTHER SEXUALLY TRANSMITTED DISEASES

49 What is gonorrhea?

Gonorrhea is a bacterial infection. The name of the bacterium is *neisseria gonorrhea*, or gonococci. The bacteria look like beans under a microscope, and usually come in pairs. These bacteria grow well in the moist inner linings of the penis, vagina, anus and throat. Therefore you can catch gonorrhea through sexual activity involving any of these areas; not only through vaginal intercourse, but also through anal intercourse and oral sex.

However, they quickly die when away from these warm, moist areas, and so cannot be caught by being in the same room with an infected person, by casual contact, or by hugging or kissing. However, if you directly touched an infected area on another person's body and then immediately touched a warm, moist area on your own body—your eyes for example—you could catch the disease. Similarly, a person already infected could spread the infection to other parts of his or her own body in the same way.

Prevention: Keeping to one sexual partner who also does not have sex with others is the best protection. The condom, used with contraceptive foam or jelly, protects against gonorrhea. It is possible that urinating soon after intercourse may sometimes kill or expel the bacteria, but it would have to be done very soon after intercourse, and is not a reliable method.

Symptoms in men: The first symptoms, which appear two to ten days after sexual contact, are a mild or severe burning during urination, and/or a discharge from the tip of the penis (the opening of the urethra). The discharge may be clear or creamy, white, yellow or green. Sometimes it is more obvious just after the man wakes up. However, about one man in five who contracts gonorrhea has no symptoms at all. Although these symptoms usually go away after awhile, the disease continues to spread.

Symptoms in women: Gonorrhea is more dangerous in women, because most women who become infected through the vagina have no symptoms. Those who do may have an increased discharge and some irritation of the vaginal lips. It is unusual for women to feel a burning sensation when urinating.

Symptoms in both men and women:

1. **Mouth infection:** People who catch gonorrhea through oral sex may experience a sore throat, but will probably not realize that this pain is due to a sexually transmitted disease. There are usually no symptoms at all for a mouth infection.

2. **Anal infection:** Usually there are no symptoms, but sometimes there is some itching or a discharge from the anus that may be bloody. As with mouth symptoms, these may go unnoticed or the person may not connect them to a sexually transmitted disease.

Women catch gonorrhea more easily from men than men catch it from women. A man who has intercourse with an infected woman has a fifty percent chance of catching it, but a woman who has intercourse with an infected man has more than a seventy percent chance of catching it. Women may also have gonorrhea spread from the vagina to the anus.

Because they are so close together, vaginal secretions can easily carry the bacteria to the anus.

Long-term effects of the disease in men: In men, gonorrhea may infect the internal organs involved in reproduction, the prostate, parts of the testicles and the tubes through which sperm travel from the testicles to the penis. This may cause scarring which may make it impossible for the man to become a father.

Long-term effects of the disease in women: The bacteria can infect the lips of the vagina causing swelling and pain. They can spread from the vagina through the cervix (the opening of the uterus) and infect the lining of the uterus and the fallopian tubes (which connect the ovaries to the uterus). By causing inflammation of these areas, they can cause pelvic inflammatory disease (PID). They may also cause scarring of the tubes. If both tubes are scarred, the woman will be unable to have children. If only one tube is scarred, she could have a fetus begin to develop in the tube instead of the uterus (ectopic pregnancy)—something that may kill her.

Long-term effects for both sexes: arthritis and meningitis (inflammation of the membranes around the brain), blindness in infants born to infected mothers, heart and liver damage, leading to death.

Symptoms of the spread of infection include lower abdominal pain, pain during sexual intercourse, increased cramping during menstruation, "spotting" between periods, irregular periods, fever, chills, weight loss and a general feeling of being sick.

It is very important to remember that gonorrhea can be spread to a baby as it is being born, and may cause the baby to become blind. Therefore, all women should be tested during pregnancy for this disease, so that precautions can be taken.

Gonorrhea is diagnosed in men by inserting a thin swab into the opening of the penis, and testing the secretions in a laboratory. Samples may also be taken from the throat or anus.

In women, the diagnosis is a little more difficult, because the symptoms are less obvious. The woman will usually be examined, and samples of the fluids of the vagina, throat and anus will be taken.

Gonorrhea is treated by giving the patient a single large dose of antibiotics. However, some varieties of the gonorrhea-causing bacteria are becoming resistant to the antibiotics and stronger doses are needed. Such resistant bacteria are more common in some large U.S. cities like New York. They are also common in parts of Asia and Africa.

People with gonorrhea must not have sex until follow-up tests show that they are cured.

50 What is syphilis?

Syphilis is an STD caused by a bacterium called *treponema pallidum.*

Symptoms: In the first stage, syphilis produces a painless, open sore called a chancre (pronounced "shanker") where it enters the body. It is usually red and solid looking, and is raised up from the skin surface. It usually appears first around the genitalia, but may also occur around the mouth or rectum. If a chancre occurs inside a woman's vagina, it may not be noticed.

In the second stage, it produces a rash of small, red, scaly bumps that do not itch, patches of mucous, gray spots in the mouth, hair loss, as well as a general feeling of sickness, including sore throat and swollen glands.

If left untreated: After the second-stage symptoms are gone, the disease may progress for years without the person being aware of anything wrong, and it is only detectable through a blood test. Years later it may reappear to produce numerous problems that may prove fatal. (Occasionally, even in the second stage it infects the liver, the eyes or the membranes covering the brain.) It can cause brain damage which in turn may cause paralysis, insanity or other problems. It can also cause heart disease.

Prevention: Knowing your sexual partners, not having more than one sexual partner or not having a partner who is having sex with other people will greatly decrease your chances of catching syphilis. The condom and spermicidal foam also protect against contracting syphilis.

Syphilis bacteria enter at the penis, vagina, throat or rectum. The disease may be transmitted by vaginal and anal intercourse as well as by oral sex, in which a part of the uninfected individual's body makes contact with the sore, rash or mucous patch. It does not live outside of the body and so can only be transmitted by direct contact.

Syphilis is diagnosed by a blood test. It can be treated with antibiotics such as penicillin.

51 What is chlamydia?

Chlamydia is caused by the chlamydia trachomatis, a bacteria-like organism. It grows well in the moist lining of the penis, vagina, rectum and mouth, and may be spread by vaginal and anal intercourse, as well as oral sex.

Prevention: The condom and spermicidal foam protect against Chlamydia. As with other STDs, knowing your partner, and restricting the number of partners you have will reduce your chances of infection.

Symptoms in women: An itching and burning in the vaginal area are common. A watery, whitish vaginal discharge, a dull and long-lasting pain in the pelvic area, "spotting" between periods or a low fever are frequent symptoms. However, more than three-quarters of infected women have no early symptoms.

Symptoms in men: A watery, whitish discharge from the penis, painful urination, burning or itching around the opening of the penis may all be symptoms of chlamydia. Pain in the testicles is another symptom. About one man in ten with the disease has no symptoms until long after the disease has started.

Symptoms in both men and women: A whitish, watery discharge from anus.

Long-term effects of the disease: Chlamydia may lead to pelvic inflammatory disease (PID) which can damage the woman's fallopian tubes. It also increases the risk of still-birth and miscarriage. Newborn babies who contract Chlamydia can have eye, ear and lung infections. Chlamydia can be successfully treated with antibiotics.

52 What is herpes? How can you tell if you have it? What does it mean to have a sore vagina?

Herpes is an STD caused by a virus called herpes simplex virus 2 (HSV 2). Once it enters the body, the virus travels to nearby nerve cells. Doctors have no way of eliminating it at present. Like the chicken pox virus, it never leaves the body. However, in healthy people it does no serious damage, although people with weakened immune systems may suffer serious infections from HSV viruses.

Symptoms: The main negative effect is painful blisters. It is through these blisters that herpes is recognized. They form two to twenty days after infection; on average after six days. First, tiny blisters appear on the skin or a moist membrane. On the male genitalia, they can appear on the round tip of the penis, the foreskin or the shaft. They form occasionally in the urethra. On the female genitalia, they may appear on the lips of the vagina, the interior walls of the vagina which may cause intercourse to be painful, on the cervix (entrance to the uterus) where they may cause no pain but can produce a watery discharge. They may also form around the anus or on and around the mouth.

Soon after they form, the blisters rupture and form shallow ulcers (sores) that sometimes have a greyish covering. Eventually they dry up and a scab is formed. Finally the scab falls off, usually without leaving any scarring. These blisters are extremely painful. Touching them, the pressure of clothing, sexual activity can also cause intense pain. If urine touches a blister, it can cause a severe burning sensation.

If you have a small blister anywhere on your body and you don't know what caused it, or you feel pain in your sexual organs, you need to check with a doctor. A woman won't be able to see the blisters inside her vagina, but she will feel pain. The sores may be on her cervix where she does not feel pain, but she may have a watery discharge.

Prevention: Herpes travel from one person to another more easily than most other STDs. It enters the person's body at the penis, vagina, mouth, eyes and anus, and can be spread by sexual intercourse or just by touching an infected area and then touching one of these openings. So simply by touching another person's sexual organs you can catch herpes.

You can also spread herpes from one part of your body to another by touching the blisters. Herpes is especially dangerous for the eyes. If you think you have touched herpes blisters, it is very important to wash your hands thoroughly, as well as any other part of your body that you may have touched. It is also a good idea to avoid using other people's towels, because a warm, moist towel may transfer the herpes virus.

However, it is the blisters that give off the virus, although some virus may be given off by the skin shortly before they appear. For this reason, herpes is unlikely to be spread by contact once the blisters have cleared up.

The first appearance of the blisters after infection is often the worst. They may take three weeks or longer to clear up. Flu-like symptoms of fever, aching, chills and tiredness can appear. The lymph nodes near the infected area—e.g. in the groin—can swell.

Subsequent appearances of the blisters are usually less severe. They last only about seven to ten days, and flu symptoms are less common. This is because the body produces antibodies to the HSV 2 virus. There may be recurrences several times a year, once a year, or never. Recurrences often become less frequent as time goes on and the body builds up greater resistance. Getting adequate rest, eating properly, cutting down on smoking and drinking may increase resistance to the disease and reduce the likelihood and severity of future outbreaks. Exposure to sunlight, fever, emotional stress, injuries and menstruation may trigger a recurrence.

Treatment of outbreaks consists of keeping the infected areas clean and dry, and by avoiding intimate contact with others. Bacteria may infect the blisters, making them more painful and delaying healing.

There is a medication called acyclovir that helps reduce the blisters' soreness and makes them heal sooner. Acyclovir capsules may also help to reduce the number of outbreaks. You may hear of other ointments, but these should be avoided unless recommended by a doctor. Other ointments may keep the blisters moist and actually prolong their presence; ointments with steroids may also retard healing. Warm baths, followed by drying the skin with a hair dryer can reduce discomfort.

There are also support groups for herpes sufferers to help them learn how to live with the disease, keep it under control and avoid spreading it to others.[6]

53 Can you catch herpes from a toilet seat?

No, you can only get it by having sexual intercourse or by touching the herpes sores on another person's genitals, mouth, or anus while the disease is active (as indicated by the presence of blisters or sores).

54 Is there a test for herpes?

Yes there is. Fluids are taken from the blisters and tested in a laboratory to confirm the diagnosis.

55 If you have herpes, can you have a child?

Yes you can. However, special care is necessary because a baby may suffer brain damage or even die from a herpes infection. A man with herpes should avoid having intercourse with his wife when the blisters are present. A woman with herpes needs to inform the doctor who will deliver the baby that she has the disease. Even if she has had a sore on her vagina only one time, she must tell her doctor. She should also tell her doctor if she has ever experienced vaginal pain, as this might mean she had herpes blisters inside her vagina.

A woman infected with herpes usually will not give it to the fetus directly through the bloodstream; her own antibodies to herpes will protect the fetus too. (However, a first-time infection with herpes occurring during pregnancy runs a higher risk of infecting the fetus since the mother's body has not yet formed antibodies.)

The main danger is that the baby may contract the disease during birth, but a doctor who knows ahead of time may be able to protect the baby. If the blisters break out right before the baby is due, it can be delivered by Caesarean delivery (see CAESAREAN DELIVERY in the glossary). This way, it may not come in contact with the blisters because it does not pass through the cervix and vagina.

56 What is hepatitis?

Hepatitis is an inflammation of the liver. There are three kinds that can be transmitted sexually: hepatitis A, hepatitis B and hepatitis non-A non-B. Hepatitis A is caused by a virus that may be transmitted by contact with fecal material. Sexual activity involving contact with the anus and rectum can therefore transmit it. Hepatitis B may be transferred by contact with most bodily fluids, including saliva, semen, urine, feces and blood. Hence it can be transferred sexually, by use of an infected person's toothbrush, razor, nail clippers, thermometer, etc.

Hepatitis A is the least serious of these diseases; it usually heals by itself. Hepatitis B also usually heals by itself, but it may linger as a chronic disease with mild symptoms, and damage the liver.

The symptoms are fatigue, muscle and joint pain, sore throat, abdominal pain, fever, nausea and vomiting. The feces may turn pale, the urine dark or orange and jaundice (yellowing of the skin and of the whites of the eyes) may develop.

The presence and type of hepatitis is determined by blood tests. Treatment consists of rest, proper diet and the avoidance of drugs and alcohol. Immune globulin can protect against Hepatitis A, and there is now a vaccine for Hepatitis B. People traveling to countries where Hepatitis A is common should take immune globulin, and people at risk of catching Hepatitis B, such as male homosexuals, should receive the vaccine.

57 What is vaginitis? What is a yeast infection? What is trichomoniasis ("trich")? What is Gardnerella?

Vaginitis is a general term for several irritating infections of the vagina that may be transmitted by close physical contact, including sexual contact. There are two different types: trichomoniasis and gardnerella. All of them, if left untreated in women, may cause serious pelvic infections.

Yeast infections are caused by a fungus. The main symptoms are a thick, cheese-like vaginal discharge, itching and skin irritation. Treatment includes medication which must be prescribed by a doctor.

Trichomonaisis is caused by a tiny, one-celled creature called "trichomonas vaginalis." It is a type of protozoa. Its most common symptom is a fairly strong discharge that can be white, yellowish or greenish. It may be frothy. The discharge itself may cause irritation of the vaginal lips, making them sore and itchy. Urination may cause a burning sensation. The trichomonaisis protozoa is easily visible under the microscope in fluid secretions taken from the vagina. It is oval shaped and has 4 tail-like strings attached at one end which propel it forward. It is transmitted sexually but may also be caught from a public bath, and for this reason a woman with the disease should avoid sharing baths with others.

It is usually treated with the antibiotic metronidazole, known by the brand name Flagyl, but there is some controversy over whether this drug is entirely safe, especially if a woman uses it repeatedly. It should probably be avoided for the first three months of pregnancy and during breastfeeding. Iodine douches can be used instead. If you have "trich" you may want to contact a woman's health care center in your area to find out current thinking about treatment of the disease. The disease itself will not harm babies.

Men can also catch this disease and they should seek medical care for proper treatment. Men who have the disease should abstain from intercourse or use condoms with spermicide until the disease has left.

Gardnerella, also known as clue cells or hemophilus, is caused by bacteria. Its main symptom is a whitish grey fishy-smelling discharge from the vagina. Gardnerella may clear up without treatment, but is usually treated with antibiotics.

58 What is crabs?

"Crabs" is a slang term for an infestation of lice called crab lice or pthirus pubis. They live on the hairy parts of the body: the pubic hair, the hair around the anus, under the arms, on the chest, in a man's beard and occasionally on the head. They look like tiny crabs under a magnifying glass. You can recognize them yourself—if you see tiny dots that move, either grey or brownish red, then you have crabs.

They can be transferred through sexual or other direct physical contact. But they can also survive away from a person for as much as forty-eight hours, and may also be transferred indirectly—for example they can be picked up from bed sheets and blankets.

The usual treatment is to apply the drug gamma benzene hexachloride, sold under the names Lindane®, Kwell® and Kwellada® to the affected parts of the body. You need a doctor's prescription for it in the United States, but not in Canada. It should be used sparingly with children, as it has been known to cause convulsions in young children. Other pest-killing drugs are available without prescription, such as Rid and Spraypax. You might ask your pharmacist. Vaseline rather than a drug should be used around the eyes. Pregnant or breastfeeding women should **not** use gamma benzene hexachloride (Lindane, Kwell or Kwellada).

59 What are scabies?

Scabies is a disease in which tiny mites, called sarcoptes scabei, infest the skin of the hands, arms, feet, ankles, genitals, buttocks and armpits. The female mite burrows into the skin, lays eggs and dies. The most common symptom is itching, which is an allergic reaction to the mite.

Like crabs, scabies may be transferred not only through direct intimate contact, but through contact with clothing, furniture, bed sheets and sometimes even pet animals.

The treatment is also gamma benzene hexachloride. See the discussion of this drug under treatment of crab lice, above. Another drug used is crotamiton sold under the brand name Eurax. Sulfur ointment is also used.

60 What are veneral warts?

Veneral warts (their medical name is *condylomat acuminata*) appear around the sex organs and anus. They often begin as small lumps with an irregular, cauliflower-like surface.

They are caused by a virus called "human papilloma virus" or HPV, a virus similar to other wart-causing viruses. They are mainly spread by close contact of warm and moist areas of the body, i.e. through vaginal and anal intercourse and oral sex. They can also be carried from one part of the body to another by bodily secretions.

In women, they most often appear on the vaginal lips, in the space between the vagina and the anus, but also inside the vagina, on the cervix (entrance to the uterus), on the anus or in the rectum.

In men, they usually appear on the rounded tip of the penis (the glans), the foreskin and at the opening of the urethra (place where urine comes out of the penis). They can also appear on the shaft of the penis, on the scrotum, by the anus or in the rectum. Men can also have small shiny spots on the glans called "pearly papules;" these are not warts, but a normal part of the penis. If you are in doubt, check with a doctor.

In both men and women they can also appear in the throat.

Symptoms: Aside from the presence of the warts themselves, itching and irritation are common.

If left untreated they can become large enough to block the vagina, anus or throat. Treatment of external warts usually involves application of the drug podophyllin directly to the warts. It is a strong chemical which may cause burns to healthy skin, which is usually protected with vaseline. There is controversy about whether it should be used for internal warts because it is so strong. Podophyllin may cause fetal damage and should not be used during pregnancy. Alternative treatments involve freezing the warts with liquid nitrogen, and electric cauterization or burning the warts with a laser. Occasionally surgery may be necessary.

Treatment of these warts may take some patience, because while the visible warts are being treated, new ones emerge that were previously missed. The warts often take a long time to appear, and repeat treatments may be necessary. Sexual partners should use condoms during sex until the warts have definitely eradicated.

There is some evidence that infection with the HPV virus increases a woman's chances of developing cervical cancer, so a woman who has had venereal warts should be sure to have regular pap smears. Regular pap smears are a good practice for any woman who wants to maintain good health.

REFERENCES

1. Hatcher, R.; Guest, Falicia; Stewart, G.; Trussell, James; Bowen, S. C.; Cates, W. *Contraceptive Technology.* New York: Irvington Publishers, 1988, pp. 16–18.
2. Boston Women's Health Book Collective. *Our Bodies Ourselves.* New York: Simon and Schuster, 1976, p. 168.
3. Ibid. (Hatcher) p. 15.
4. Ibid. (Hatcher) p. 17.
5. Ibid. (Hatcher) p. 4.
6. Felman, Y. M. & Hoke, A. W. *Wellcome Atlas Of Sexually Transmitted Diseases.* Triangle Park, N.C.: Burroughs Wellcome Co., 1985, pp. 10–13.

Chapter VI

HEREDITY

1 What physical characteristics are inherited?

All of our physical characteristics are inherited from our parents. The shape of the nose, the shape and color of the eyes, height, the size and shape of the hands and feet are all inherited. In fact, the fundamental qualities that make us human are inherited; the structures of our organs, our ability to think and to speak, to walk upright and so forth.

However, environment also has a strong effect on your growth and development. For example, someone who has genes to be tall, but does not eat adequately while growing up, will probably not be as tall as his genes could have made him. An architect's plans are of little value if there are not enough wooden beams, too few bricks or too little mortar to carry them out.

2 Are some people more intelligent than others because they have better genes?

There is much disagreement now as to whether there are significant inborn differences in intelligence from one person to another. (Inborn traits are traits we have from birth, that are determined only by our genes). Of course the genes that make us human beings—and not squirrels— make us a lot smarter than squirrels! Some people are clearly mentally disabled and have less innate ability than the rest of us. But most scientists agree that environment, attitude and interest are very strong influences on intelligence, and that it is quite possible for you to go to college and become a famous doctor, teacher, scientist or astronaut, even if your parents never finished high school.

3 Why do some people do so much better in school than others?

Some young people take learning much more seriously than others. While their friends are watching television, they are reading or are out looking at nature, visiting museums, experimenting with scientific toys or playing stimulating games. Some people are more fortunate than others in that their families have more money and can send them to better schools where they attend smaller classes and receive more indi-

171

vidual attention. Others may have had to quit school early to support their parents, spouses or children.

But even parents who may lack education can encourage their children to study. With the many public libraries, museums, clubs and hobby organizations around, even a child of parents with low incomes can excel in learning. Try watching only educational programs on TV and limit yourself to two hours TV a day for a month. Start reading more and take up active hobbies during the rest of the time. You may be surprised to see how much smarter you have become in such a short time!

If you have children of your own, you can help them reach their full capacity by providing a rich, stimulating environment for them from birth on. This does not mean spending a lot of money for fancy toys. It does mean listening to them when they first attempt to talk, showing them interesting things like leaves, birds and animals you see around where you live and encouraging them when they themselves pick up some interesting object and look at it.

By asking questions, children are showing their own natural intelligence and curiosity. If, instead of becoming impatient and angry you encourage your child's curiosity while protecting him or her from danger, you will set your child on the right track of following his or her curiosity and loving to learn new things.

4 Are there specific things that determine such features as hair color and eye color?

Yes. Each of our cells contains a complete set of instructions for all our physical characteristics. These instructions are called genes. An estimated 50,000 and 100,000 genes form the complete set. Together, your genes form something like an architect's plans for constructing you down to the last detail.

5 How do you inherit your parents' characteristics, like looks, hair color or body frame?

We receive half of our genes from our mothers, half from our fathers. The father's share is in the sperm, the mother's in the egg (ovum). They combine when the ovum and sperm come together to start a new person; together, the two sets of genes together determine all our physical characteristics.

Your parents in turn received their genes from their parents, and so on back through hundreds of generations. So you are carrying genes from your grandparents, great grandparents—indeed from people who lived thousands of years ago—and you have some of their physical characteristics!

Although we receive all our genes from our parents, some of the characteristics may not have been apparent in them. For example, you might have red hair while your mother and father both have brown hair.

6 What is the difference between chromosomes and genes?

Chromosomes are long strings which hold the genes. You might think of the genes as the words of a book giving the instructions for how you are to be. The chromosomes are the chapters, each containing many words. The 50,000 to 100,000 genes are attached to forty-six chromosomes in human beings. They form twenty-three pairs. Each pair consists of one chromosome from the mother, and one chromosome from the father.

Different living things have different numbers of chromosomes—a cat has thirty-eight, a frog twenty-six, a mushroom twelve. Two genes, one on each chromosome control a certain characteristic—hair color, height, the shape of the nose, and so forth.[1]

7 Where are genes and chromosomes located? How do they function?

The chromosomes, containing the genes, are located in the center of the cell, in a part called the nucleus. They are composed of a chemical called deoxyribonucleic acid, or DNA. The DNA gives instructions to the cell on how to grow by sending out another chemical called messenger ribonucleic acid or RNA, which puts the blueprint contained in the DNA into action.

DNA consists of only four basic chemicals; it is the order in which these four chemicals are arranged that makes up the genetic code or instructions. The DNA in each and every cell is identical and holds the entire pattern for all your characteristics. It is theoretically possible that one cell from your body could be used to produce another person exactly like you in every bodily characteristic, although it is scientifically impossible to achieve this at this time.

We know that a computer chip can now be made that is very small but contains all the information of a complete book. A human cell is similar. It is so small it can only be seen through a microscope, but it contains information about you that would fill several books!

8 What determines whether a baby will be a girl or a boy?

As with all other characteristics, a baby's gender is controlled by two genes on a pair of chromosomes. While in most pairs of chromosomes the two members of the pair look alike, this is not the case for the chromosomes holding the sex genes. Under the microscope, scientists can easily tell the sex of a person by looking at these chromosomes. If the baby receives two X chromosomes—X–X—then it will be a girl. If it receives one X and one Y chromosome—X–Y—then it will be a boy.

The mother only gives the baby an X chromosome, because all her cells contain only X chromosomes. Her egg cells also contain only an X chromosome. But the father provides the new baby with either an X or a Y chromosome. Because each of his sperm contain either an X chromosome or a Y chromosome, the father determines the baby's sex. There are millions of sperm with X chromosomes and millions of sperm with Y chromosomes. It is chance that decides which type reaches the egg first! In some kinds of animals—birds for example—the female determines the sex of the baby.

9 How is it that a baby can have red hair, while its mother and father have dark hair? What is meant by a recessive or dominant trait?

There are two genes for each characteristic—like eye color or skin color—and one comes from each parent. These are called "traits." The two genes do not always "agree" in the instructions they give. One gene might instruct the eyes to become brown, the other gene might tell them to become blue. One gene is recessive, the other is dominant. For example the gene for red hair is recessive. This means if the gene for red hair is from one parent and the gene for brown hair is from the other, the person will have brown hair. The dominant gene (brown hair) overrules the recessive gene (red hair). The dominant gene is "expressed" while the recessive gene is "unexpressed." If the child receives two recessive genes for red hair—then the recessive genes are expressed. That is why two people with brown hair may have a red-haired child—each parent carried one recessive gene for red hair and one dominant gene for brown hair. The genes for red hair remained inactive in both parents, but when the two genes for red hair came together in the child, the child developed red hair.

This is also the reason that parents may be carriers of a genetically transmitted disease but not have the disease themselves.

THE INHERITANCE OF RECESSIVE GENES

```
        MOTHER           FATHER
        D   R             D   R

    CHILD  CHILD      CHILD  CHILD
     D  D   D  R       R  D   R  R*
            +          +
```

D = Dominant Gene, R = Recessive Gene.

The child with the recessive characteristic is marked '*'.

The children who carry the recessive characteristic and may pass it on to their children are marked '+'.

If only one parent carried the recessive gene, none of the children would have the characteristic, but two out of four—fifty percent—would carry it.

10 What are some diseases that are hereditary?

Color blindness is inherited. So is hemophilia, an inability for the blood to clot. The chromosomes for these diseases are carried by women, but men usually are the ones who have the disease.[1] Color blindness is not a serious disease, and hemophilia can be treated very successfully.

Some hereditary diseases can take years to appear, like Huntington's chorea, a disease in which the brain and nervous system start to degenerate around the age of forty or fifty years. If there is no history of this disease in your family, you should not worry about developing it.

We also know there are inherited tendencies. This means that a person may inherit an increased probability of contracting a disease, like diabetes or heart disease. (Such tendencies usually depend upon the complex interaction of many different genes.) But the conditions you experience after birth may also affect whether you will contract the disease or not. For example, if you have an increased tendency for heart disease, you should be careful not to eat fatty foods and exercise regularly. If you have an increased tendency for diabetes, you should avoid eating large amounts of sugar and starches. Eating well, regular exercise, not smoking, not drinking excessively, not taking drugs, prevent many diseases, including those for which you may have an inherited tendency.

There are also diseases caused by genetic changes or damage, where the damage happens either to the sperm and ovum, or to the fetus's chromosomes early in its development. In Down's syndrome, a form of mental retardation, there is an extra chromosome in one set—three

---

[1]This is because the genes that produce these diseases are recessive, and are on the X chromosome. In a woman, the other X chromosome in her X-X pair will probably be normal. But in a man, the Y chromosome is shorter than the X chromosome, and has no counterbalancing genes for these traits.

instead of two. This chromosome may have come from a defective sperm or ovum, but most of the parents' body cells, including their sperm and ova, did not have this defect.

Cancer may also occur in this way. Somehow the genes in one or a few cells are damaged so that they begin to reproduce erratically. This genetic damage did not come from the parent, and it may not be passed along to the cancer patient's children. Such damage may be caused by harmful chemicals in the environment—tar and nicotine in cigarette smoke are the most common examples; and some pesticides are also known to cause genetic damage leading to cancer.

11 Why is it bad to have sex with a close relative? Why are the children of a man and woman who are also closely related by blood often retarded?

Most defective or bad genes are recessive, so it usually takes two bad genes for the defect to be expressed. If two people who marry each other are closely related by blood, they have many genetic characteristics in common. If the husband has a gene that produces a defect, such as one for retardation, it is much more likely that the wife will also have this same "bad" gene than if they were not related.

It is common knowledge that marrying close relatives increases the risk of disease among any children that are born. Many members of European royal families suffered from hemophilia because their families had a long tradition of only marrying people from other royal families. Before long, most of Europe's rulers were closely related to each other, and this genetic disease was frequent among Europe's elite.

During World War II, a small tribe was discovered in the Philippines that was totally isolated from other people. Half of them were albino— their skin color and eye color were very light. Their extreme isolation meant that they could only marry each other, so this genetically caused characteristic spread to half of the total population.

Two close relatives are more likely to have the same defective gene than two people who are not related, because they are descended from the same people. Suppose you marry your first cousin. Your first cousin is the child of your uncle or aunt—let's say your uncle for this example. Your uncle is your uncle because he is your mother's or father's brother— let's say your mother's brother.

Both your mother and her brother had the same parents. That means that you and your cousin had the same two grandparents. If only one of your grandparents had a defective gene, and you married your first cousin, there is a good chance that you both carry that bad gene. Most genetic diseases need two genes for the disease to occur (that is, the defective gene is recessive). But if both you and your partner carry the gene there is a strong chance—one in four—that any child of yours will have the genetic disease, even though neither you nor your partner, nor your parents or grandparents, had the disease. If you and your cousin each marry someone else, it is much less likely that the people you marry will carry the same bad gene.

12 What are mutations?

Mutations are changes in the genes. Through mutations, a child may have genes giving it a characteristic which its parents' genes did not have. For example, the child might be mentally retarded through Downs's syndrome even though neither of its parents had the genes for retardation. Down's syndrome is far more common in children born to women over the age of thirty-five years. Amniocentesis may be performed while the fetus is still very young to test for different types of genetically transmitted diseases, including mutations. (See AMNIOCENTESIS in the Glossary.)

We do not know all the causes for gene mutations, but one cause is radiation. We are most familiar with radiation from nuclear power plants and atomic weapons, but there is also a certain amount of naturally occurring radiation all around us.

Most mutations cause deformities that make an animal or human being less able to survive than its parents. But some encourage improved survival. For example, the first one-celled animals may have been insensitive to light. But through a mutation, somewhere along the line one of the animals may have become sensitive to light, and this helped it survive—perhaps by moving away from light that heated it up too much. So this creature did better than those without the mutation, and lived a bit longer. It was able to reproduce for a longer period of time. Its genes were passed on more than those of creatures insensitive to light. After many, many more chance mutations and millions of years had passed, the ability to see developed out of this initial sensitivity to light. This is how evolution takes place.

13 Why are there different races?

Human beings first appeared in the Middle East. It is thought that many hundreds of thousands of years ago, and over the course of many centuries, large numbers of people left the Middle East for Africa, Asia and Europe. Because the climates and conditions were so different in these places, they gradually developed different traits to enable them to survive better.

In northern Europe, for example, those people with lighter skin survived better, because they were better able to take in more of the thinner sunlight to manufacture Vitamin D. (They did not have fortified milk then!) However, in Africa, darker-skinned people survived better because it prevented them from producing too much Vitamin D in the bright sun.

African-Americans are susceptible to a blood disease called sickle-cell anemia. But those who carry the disease (see Question 9, above) actually gain a survival advantage from it: they are protected from malaria, a common disease of tropical climates like Africa. We don't know how every trait was helpful, but we know that it must have been.

A race consists of a group of people sharing the same physical characteristics. However, many scientists no longer think that race is a very useful biological concept, and prefer to speak simply of human variation. This is because most genes are shared by the different races. What makes races different is simply that one group is more likely to have genes that produce certain characteristics like a certain shape of nose or eyes, while another group is more likely to have genes for different characteristics. In fact, some members of each race can have many of the genetic characteristics of another race. Looked at from the point of view of genes, the once-sharp lines distinguishing one race from another have grown blurred and are sometimes impossible to determine.

14 What would happen if two sperm entered the egg at the same time?

Many people think that two fetuses would start to grow, but this is not the case. Instead, we think that the egg is destroyed. This is because there is too much genetic material. As already noted, there are forty-six chromosomes, which form twenty-three pairs ($23 \times 2 = 46$). When a new baby is conceived, one chromosome in each pair comes from the father, the other chromosome from the mother. Only twenty-three chromosomes are needed from the father. The forty-six chromosomes, in twenty-three pairs, together make up a complete set of instructions that tells the fertilized egg how to grow into a human being.

If two sperm were to enter, there would be forty-six chromosomes from the father, plus twenty-three from the mother, so the egg would have too many chromosomes containing too many genes giving too many instructions. Probably the same thing happens to the egg that would happen if two different architects made up plans for a building without talking to each other. If the workers tried to build it following both sets of plans— now this one, now that one—the building might have all windows and no walls, or a top floor built out into empty space with no support! The building would fall down long before it was fully built!

15 Can a woman become pregnant by having intercourse with another animal—a dog for example?

No, she cannot. The genetic instructions are completely incompatible. Dogs do not even have the same number of chromosomes as human beings. Some creatures may cross-breed, such as horses and asses, but this is because they have nearly identical genetic material.

16 How do the genes and chromosomes from each parent combine to give you characteristics from both parents?

As we said, the genes form strings called chromosomes. The forty-six chromosome strings lie in pairs—twenty-three of them (46 ÷ 2 = 23). You received one of each pair of your chromosomes from each parent when you were conceived—half from your mother's ovum, half from your father's sperm.

So when you received one chromosome from each pair of chromosomes from your mother, you had one complete set of instructions. But then these were joined by another complete set from your father—one chromosome from each pair of your father's chromosomes. Since that moment, you have had two complete sets of instructions on how you should be. (Remember, there are two genes for each characteristic.)

The chromosome that carried the genes for the same traits from each parent found the other one, so the two chromosomes formed a new pair. The genes on each member of a pair of chromosomes are in the same order, like two identical trains, each having an engine, mail car, baggage car, tank car, and caboose, so the two genes for each characteristic lie next to each other. Of course a chromosome has many more genes in its "train" than the longest freight train. Each pair of genes—one on each chromosome—together determines that characteristic (see Question 9, above).

17 What is the advantage to a child having two parents? Why wouldn't it work just as well for one person alone to start a new baby?

If one person could start a baby by herself or himself, the baby would be genetically identical to its parent—an identical twin. But thanks to sex, when a baby is conceived, it receives genetic material from its two parents whose chances of being identical are very tiny (unless two identical twins were to marry!). By having such material from two people, the offspring will never be exactly like either one of them—or anyone else (except an identical twin).

In fact, just two parents can produce more than 64 trillion (64,000,000,-000,000) different combinations of chromosomes.[2] This is far more than all the people who have ever lived. This great diversity enables the human race to survive better. In the Middle Ages, plagues swept through Europe—like the Black Plague of 1348—and wiped out large portions of western Europe's population, killing countless numbers of people as far away as China and Siberia. Fortunately, since almost no-one was exactly like anyone else, many people were either resistant to the disease or completely immune, and the human race survived.

Even though we have greater control over the environment and know more about fighting off diseases than we did back then, there is still the possibility that some major change could threaten our survival, as the appearance of AIDS teaches us. If the Earth's climate were to become much warmer than it is now (as many scientists think is happening), the human race would probably survive even though some of us are more suited to living in colder climates than others. But if everyone were the same, it is likely that sooner or later something would happen—a disease or a change in the environment—that would kill most or all of us, either suddenly or gradually. In addition, individual genes can be exchanged by the two chromosomes in each pair just before the sperm and egg are formed. This gives even more combinations.[2]

---

[2]There are 23 pairs of chromosomes. Each child can have either of two chromosomes from its mother, and either of two chromosomes from its father, in each pair of chromosomes. This already gives 4 possible combinations of chromosomes in just one pair. Since there are 23 pairs, there are 4×4 or (4^{23}) possible combinations!

REFERENCES

1. Calderone, M. & Johnson. E. *Family Book Of Sexuality.* New York: Bantam Books, 1983, p. 82.
2. Kelly, G. F. *Sexuality: The Human Perspective.* New York: Barron's Educational Series, 1980, p. 282.

GLOSSARY—
INCLUDING SLANG/STREET TERMS

NOTE: Terms italicized in each definition have their own glossary entries that more fully explain them.

A

ABORTION: Spontaneous abortion or miscarriage is the expulsion of a fetus from the uterus. Clinical abortion is the medical termination of a pregnancy before the fetus can survive on its own, usually within the first twelve weeks.

ABSTINENCE: Not taking part in sexual intercourse.

ADOPTION: The process whereby a couple or individual accepts the responsibility for a child that is not born to them.

ADRENOLIN: A hormone produced by the adrenal glands; may raise blood pressure or stop bleeding.

AFTERBIRTH: See *PLACENTA*.

AIDS: Acquired Immune Deficiency Syndrome; a disease that attacks the body's immune system. Is considered a sexually transmitted disease.

ALLERGIC: Hypersensitivity to a specific substance such as dust, a certain food or combination of foods, etc.

AMNIOCENTESIS: A medical test done on some pregnant women, usually older women, to determine if the baby growing inside them will be a normal baby. The test involves inserting a needle into the amniotic sack, and extracting a small amount of the amniotic fluid. From the fluid, laboratory technicians can extract a few cells that the fetus has given off. They can check to see whether their genetic material appears normal. This test is especially useful for detecting Down's Syndrome, a form of mental retardation.

If the doctors find that the baby is severely abnormal, the mother may decide to have an abortion to avoid bringing a child into the world who will suffer and be unhappy most of the time. This test can also determine the sex of the child, but that is not the main reason it is done. It carries risks of its own, so it should only be done when there is a good reason for it.

AMNIOTIC SACK: The thin membrane surrounding the fetus while it is in the uterus, that also contains amniotic fluid. It helps to protect the fetus while it is developing. Normally, it breaks shortly before birth; the pregnant woman will notice a flow of clear fluid out through her vagina.

ANTIBODIES: Various proteins in the blood that are generated in response to foreign proteins, such as a virus or bacterial infection, to neutralize and destroy them. The antibodies also may produce immunity against certain microorganisms and their toxins (or poisons).

ANAL INTERCOURSE: See ANUS.

ANUS: Opening at the lower end of the alimentary canal. Solid waste is released from this opening. It is located between the folds of the buttocks.

APHRODISIAC: Any substance that increases sexual desire or ability. Most things sold as aphrodisiacs do not really work.

ARTIFICIAL INSEMINATION: The union of sperm and ovum other than through sexual intercourse. Semen may be taken from a woman's husband, or another man if the husband is unable to provide adequate sperm. The semen is then inserted either into the vagina or into the uterus. In some procedures, the ovum is removed from the woman, and sperm and egg are united in a glass dish. See *IN-VITRO FERTILIZATION.*

B

BACTERIA: Small one-celled organisms that can live in most parts of the body. Some are responsible for diseases, but others, particularly those living in the intestines, help the body to function normally. Bacterial infections can usually be treated with antibiotics.

BAG OF WATERS: See *AMNIOTIC SACK.*

BALLS: Slang term for testicles. See *TESTICLES.*

BIRTH CANAL: Another name for the vagina. See *VAGINA.*

BIRTH CONTROL: Conception control; contraception. Method used to prevent pregnancy should sexual intercourse take place. See also CONTRACEPTION.

BIRTH DEFECT: A physical or biochemical defect (such as a cleft palate) that is present when a baby is born; it may be inherited or environmentally-induced.

BLADDER: Is located in the pelvic cavity. It holds the urine that flows from the kidneys and helps to pass it out of the body.

BLOW JOB: Slang term for a form of oral sexual activity. See *ORAL SEX*.

BLUE BABY: A "blue baby" is a baby born with a heart defect that causes an insufficient amount of blood to go to the lungs. This gives the baby's skin a bluish tinge. An opening between the two main pumping chambers of the heart fails to close, so blood travels through this opening, bypassing the lungs. This opening is supposed to close at birth. If it does not, it may be corrected through surgery and the child is expected to live a normal, healthy life.

BONER: Slang term for an erection. See *ERECTION*.

BOWEL MOVEMENT: The passing or release of solid waste from the rectum.

BREASTS: The two organs on the chest, marked by nipples. In women they are usually prominent and well-developed. They produce and store milk to nourish the baby during its first year or so of life.

BREAST KNOTS: A slight swelling and tenderness in the glands of the male chest. This takes place during puberty and is part of the male changes in the body at the time of rapid growth. This is normal and will go away with time.

BREECH BIRTH: A birth in which another part of the body other than the head is born first. It may cause additional difficulty or pain for the mother, but is not considered a serious problem.

BUTTOCKS: Two fleshy rounded parts at the back of the hops. Also called "butt" or "rump."

C

CAESAREAN DELIVERY: A delivery through surgery. After giving the mother a local or general anaesthetic, doctors open the mother's abdomen and uterus, and remove the baby—usually because there is some difficulty with the normal process of birth through the vaginal canal.

CARRIER: Someone who can transmit a disease to someone else, but may not have the disease himself or herself.

CELL: A small unit of material usually with a nucleus; all plants and animals are made up of these cells.

CELL NUCLEUS: The central region of every cell of the body. It contains the genetic instructions, the genes which form 46 chromosomes, that determine the structure and operation of all parts of the human body, and the particular characteristics which distinguish each person from every other.

CERVIX: The lower opening of the uterus, located toward the upper end of the vagina. It is usually closed tightly by a strong muscle. Through it, the sperm must enter to fertilize an ovum. Through it also comes the baby, as it begins the birth process. (At this time, the cervix dilates wide enough to allow the baby to pass through.) Finally, the menstrual blood also leaves the uterus through the cervix.

CHANCRES: Sores around or in the sexual organs. A sign of syphilis.

CHERRY: Slang term for entrance to the vagina, especially as it appears the first time the woman has intercourse. See *"POP THE CHERRY," VAGINA, and VIRGIN.*

CHLANYDIA: A sexually-transmitted disease; a bacteria; can be cured.

CHROMOSOMES: Any of the microscopic rod-shaped bodies. They carry the genes that convey hereditary characteristics. In the human, there are forty-six or twenty-three pairs.

CIRCUMCISION: A minor surgical procedure in which the foreskin of the penis is cut. Originally a religious ritual, for many years it was performed on most male newborns as a health measure. Recently, its medical value and the risks it entails have been areas of disagreement.

CLITORIS: The organ which is the center for a woman's orgasm. It is located between the lips of the vagina, above the opening of the vaginal canal. Stimulation of it, by the man's penis during intercourse, with the hand, or through oral sexual stimulation, often causes the woman to have an orgasm.

COLESTRUM: Clear fluid released from the breasts before the mother's milk begins to be produced. Contains healthy antibodies that may help the baby resist disease.

COME: See *EJACULATION.*

CONCEPTION: see *FERTILIZATION.*

CONDOM (or "rubber"): A thin covering that may be placed over the erect penis to prevent the sperm from entering the vagina during intercourse. Latex condoms also provide some protection against sexually-transmitted diseases.

CONTRACEPTION: Methods or devices used to prevent pregnancy during intercourse.

CONTRACTION: A contraction is the narrowing and tensing of the uterus during the birth process. These contractions press the baby down and out of the uterus, through the vagina, and into the outside world.

CRAMPS: Muscular contraction of the uterus before or during menstruation.

CRABS: Pubic lice. A sexually-transmitted disease that can be transferred by other means as well. Can be cured.

CRIB DEATH: See *SUDDEN INFANT DEATH SYNDROME.*

C–SECTION: Medical slang for Caesarean Section or Caesarean Delivery. See *CAESAREAN DELIVERY.*

CUM: A slang term for seminal fluid. See *SEMINAL FLUID.*

D

D and C: Short for Dilation and Curetage. See *DILATION AND CURETAGE.*

DEFECATION: The ridding of solid waste from the body.

DIAPHRAGM: A small rubber disk that is placed into the vagina to securely cover the cervix; used as a method of birth control.

DICK, DICKIE: A slang term for penis. See *PENIS.*

DILATION: The expansion of the cervix during the birth process so that the baby can pass through.

DILATION AND CURETAGE: A surgical procedure in which the opening of the cervix is widened—dilated—and the lining of the uterus is scraped off. It is often done if a woman has abnormal bleeding, and after a miscarriage.

DISCHARGE: Release of a fluid from the body as a matter from a sore or from an opening of the body.

DNA: DNA is short for deoxyribonucleic acid. DNA is the fundamental substance that forms the genes, and contains the information that tells the body how to grow, what characteristics it is to have.

DOMINANT GENE: For each human characteristic, there is a pair of genes. The dominant gene is the one which will "overrule" another gene that gives different instructions. Dark hair is dominant over blond hair, brown eyes over blue.

DOWN'S SYNDROME: A form of mental retardation caused by an extra chromosome.

E

EATING HER OUT: Slang term for a form of oral sexual activity. See *ORAL SEX.*

ECTOPIC PREGNANCY: A pregnancy in which the fetus settles outside the uterus, often in one of the fallopian tubes, rather than in the uterus. It can be life-threatening and must be terminated.

EJACULATION: The forceful expulsion of semen, containing sperm, from the male penis. The sperm travel from the testicles to the prostate gland where the seminal fluid is added, then through the penis and out of the body.

EPISIOTOMY: A cut or incision at the opening of the vagina. This is made during the delivery of a baby to avoid the tearing in this area. Many women do not need this cut.

ERECTION: A change in the penis in which it becomes long and very firm, so that it may penetrate a woman's vagina. It is caused by a partial restriction of the blood flow out of the penis.

EVOLUTION: The development of a species from its original to its present state.

EXPRESSED GENE: A gene which has an influence in determining a bodily characteristic.

F

FAG: A derogatory slang term for homosexual. See *HOMOSEXUAL.*

FALLOPIAN TUBES: The two tubes located in the lower part of a woman's body. They are attached to the ovaries at one end and to the uterus at the other. They receive the ovum or egg from the ovaries and move it down to the uterus. If sperm are present and enter the egg, the resulting pregnancy begins in the tubes.

FECES: Waste matter expelled from the bowels; excrement.

FEMININE: Looking and acting like a female or woman.

FERTILE: The condition of an ovum or sperm which will success-fully create a baby when united in the woman's fallopian tubes; the ability of a woman to produce a child.

FERTILIZATION: The union of a sperm and ovum, which begins development of a new human being.

FETUS: The developing baby inside the uterus.

FINGERING HERSELF: This is a slang term for female masturbation. See *MASTURBATION.*

FOAM: A product used as a contraceptive. It is inserted into the vagina to help prevent pregnancy.

FOREPLAY: The activity of sexual touching, including kissing and gently touching many parts of the body, especially the breasts and sexual organs, prior to sexual intercourse.

FORESKIN: A skin that covers the head of the penis and can be retracted to uncover the tip; if the man has been circumcized, it will not be very noticeable.

FUCK, FUCKING: A slang term that means making love, mating or having intercourse. But this word is often used by someone who is angry, usually to make someone else feel bad. It gives people the wrong idea that people make love or have intercourse mainly because they are angry. The truth is that most of the time people have intercourse because they like each other very much. They are not at all angry at each other! If you want to talk about sex, it's much better to use the terms "making love," "mating," "having intercourse," or "having sex." These words let everyone know how joyful and loving sex is. See *INTERCOURSE.*

G

GARDNERELLA: A sexually-transmitted disease with a "fishy" smell; can be cured.

GAY: A popular term for homosexual, but a word not considered derogatory by most homosexuals.

GENDER: The classification of humans into male and female.

GENES: Material that is part of the cell. It contains the set of instructions for the development of the child.

GENETIC CODE: An arrangement of four chemicals that make up DNA. See DNA.

GENETIC DAMAGE: Damage done to the sperm or ovum, or fetus (unborn child) caused by a number of things, such as harmful chemicals in the environment, radiation or the contraction of a disease by the mother during pregnancy. It is not known what causes some forms of genetic damage to the child.

GENETIC DISEASE OR DISORDER: A disease or disorder carried by one or both parents that may be passed to the child through the egg and/or sperm.

GENITALIA (GENITALS): The sex organs of the male or female.

GESTATION: The period of time during which a baby is formed in the uterus, beginning with conception or fertilization, and ending with birth. Normally, it is nine months.

GONORHEA: A sexually transmitted disease. Can be cured.

H

HARD ON: A slang term for an erection. See *ERECTION.*

HEMOPHILIA: Inability of the blood to clot; an inherited disease.

HEPATITIS: A sexually-transmitted disease that causes an inflammation of the liver; can be cured. May also be contracted through other methods.

HEREDITY: The transmission from parent to offspring of certain characteristics; the tendency of the child to resemble its parents or ancestors.

HERPES SIMPLEX: A virus which may cause genital herpes, an often painful sexually transmitted disease, but one which does no known serious harm. There is no cure, but symptoms may be alleviated.

HETEROSEXUAL: A person who is sexually attracted to a member of the opposite sex.

HIV VIRUS: The virus which causes acquired immune deficiency syndrome (AIDS), a usually fatal disease. It is transmitted through sexual intercourse, oral sex, sharing of needles used to take illegal drugs, and other activities in which exchange of blood or some other bodily fluids takes place. It cannot be transmitted by being in the same room with an infected person, hugging, kissing, sharing food or dishes, or from a wet toilet seat.

HOMO: This is a slang and derogatory term for homosexual.

HOMOSEXUAL: Someone who feels sexual attraction primarily for members of his own sex. A homosexual may engage in many forms of sexual activity with other members of his or her own sex. A female homosexual is called a lesbian.

Homosexuality was formerly considered a disease or psychological disorder. But more recently it is becoming accepted as a form of sexual expression that may be more satisfying for some people than sex with a member of the opposite sex.

HORMONE: A hormone is a chemical in the body that is secreted by a gland, travels through the bloodstream to specific organs, where it has a certain effect. For example, adrenalin is produced by the adrenal glands located on the kidneys. When it is released, usually by fear or anger, it travels through the blood to the heart and stimulates it to beat faster, among other effects.

Hormones are very important to sexual functioning. The hormones estrogen and progesterone turn a woman's menstrual periods on and off by their effects on the uterus, and also cause eggs to ripen in her ovaries. The hormone testosterone causes sperm to develop, and is also responsible for causing a boy to turn into a man at puberty.

HORNY: Slang expression for experiencing sexual feelings.

HTLV-3: Another name for the AIDS virus or HIV. See *HIV.*

HYMEN: The membrane partially covering the entrance to the vaginal canal, also called the maidenhead. It may be broken during the woman's first experience of sexual intercourse, and so is considered evidence that a woman is no longer a virgin. However, it may also break during vigorous physical activity, and is not a reliable way to tell if a woman is a virgin.

HYSTERECTOMY: A surgical operation in which the only the uterus (partial hysterectomy) or both the uterus and the ovaries (complete hysterectomy) are removed. This may be for many reasons, including excessive or very painful menstrual periods, as well as many diseases. Many people, including medical personnel, feel that more hysterectomies are performed than are really necessary; it is advisable to always obtain a second opinion for surgical procedures.

I

IMMUNE GLOBULIN: Medication given to help the immune system protect against disease.

IMMUNE SYSTEM: The body system that protects against disease or helps the body recover from a disease.

IMPLANTATION: The attachment of the fetus to the lining of the uterus.

IMPOTENCE: A condition in which the male is unable to have an erection adequate for sexual intercourse. It is almost always due to emotional difficulties, not physical disease.

INCEST: Intercourse between close family members. This is against the law in all states.

INCUBATOR: A special compartment that helps babies survive who were born before the full nine month period, or who are underdeveloped. It protects the baby from infection, and enables it to have closely regulated conditions. See also *PREMATURE BABY.*

INFATUATION: Attraction that may be of short duration.

INFERTILITY: A man or woman who cannot produce healthy sperm or ova to create a child. A woman is said to have infertile periods during her menstrual cycle.

INFLAMMATION: A condition caused by virus or germ infection to some part of the body.

INHERITED TENDENCIES: An increased probability of contracting a disease or condition.

INHERITED TRAITS: See HEREDITY.

INSTINCT: Inborn tendency to behave a certain way; an automatic response to stimuli, such as sucking.

INTERCOURSE: Sexual activity that involves placing the erect penis into the vagina. This activity may result in pregnancy or contracting a sexually transmitted disease. See *MATING, MAKING LOVE, HAVING SEX.*

INTESTINES: Long tube in the lower part of the body connected to the stomach. It takes the partially digested food from the stomach and helps the body to absorb the nutrients. It also helps the body eliminate waste.

INTIMATE BODY CONTACT: Contact between two persons, such as in intercourse.

INTRAVENOUS: Into a vein.

IUD: Abbreviation for Intrauterine device. See *INTRAUTERINE DEVICE.*

INTRAUTERINE DEVICE: A small object placed inside the uterus to prevent the woman from becoming pregnant. It is not known exactly how these devices prevented conception. The IUD is rarely used today as an effective form of contraception, due to the many problems experienced by former IUD users.

IN–VITRO FERTILIZATION: Fertilization of an ovum by a sperm that takes place in a glass dish in a laboratory. It is often used to start a baby when there is some medical problem preventing the woman from beginning one inside her own body. After the fetus has begun to grow, it is inserted into its mother's uterus.

J-K

JACKING OFF, JERKING OFF: These are slang terms for male masturbation, or handling of the penis. It derives from "ejaculation," which occurs when the white fluid called the semen, which contains the sperm, is forcefully pushed from the body through the penis. See *MASTURBATION.*

KIDNEYS: Either of a pair of organs which separates water and waste products from the blood and excrete them as urine through the bladder and urethra.

L

LABIA: The lips of the vagina that surround and cover the entrance to the vaginal canal. There are two sets.

LABOR: The process preceeding birth, in which the uterus pushes the baby out of the uterus, through the birth canal and into the outside world by repeatedly contracting over the course of several hours.

LESBIAN: A female homosexual. See *HOMOSEXUAL.*

LUBRICATION: Substance used with birth control methods to increase comfort and effectiveness, such as K–Y jelly.

LYMPH NODES: Gland-like structures in the body. Part of the immune system.

M

MAIDENHEAD: See *HYMEN.*

MAMMALS: Animals and humans that nurse their young, opposed to animals that are born from eggs.

MAMMARY GLANDS: See *BREASTS.*

MAMMOGRAPHY: A specialized x-ray used to determine the health of a woman's breasts. Very small lumps (about the size of a pinhead) may be identified in this manner and provide both the woman and her doctor with early warnings of precancerous conditions.

MASCULINE: Looking and acting like a man.

MASTURBATION: Masturbation is the handling or stroking of the genitals. Sometimes this is called self-pleasuring. The penis in the man, the clitoris and vagina in women, are very sensitive and it feels good to touch or rub them. Even little babies do it.

MENARCHE: The onset of menstruation, occurring during puberty, around the ages of ten to sixteen years.

MENOPAUSE: The ending of menstruation occurring usually when a woman is in her late forties or early fifties.

MENSTRUATION: The monthly process by which a woman's uterus rids itself of dead cells and a small amount of blood through the vagina. This material, had the woman become pregnant, would have nurtured the growing fetus. However, if pregnancy does not occur, the material is expelled approximately ten days to two weeks after ovulation (the production of an egg by the ovaries).

MOLESTATION: Improper sexual activity between two individuals.

MONO: Slang for mononucleosis. See *MONONUCLEOSIS.*

MONONUCLEOSIS: "Mono," "kissing disease." A disease characterized by a fever and enlargement of the lymph nodes.

MUCUS MEMBRANE: Fluid lining body cavities and canals, such as the mouth, vagina, etc. Moistens and protects these areas.

MUTATION: A variation in some inherited trait. It may cause a defect in the baby.

N

NAVEL: Also called "belly button." A scar located in the middle of the stomach. The umbilical cord was attached to this spot, connecting the mother and baby inside her body. This cord was cut away after the birth of the child.

NOCTURNAL EMISSIONS: Also called "wet dreams." The release of sperm and semen from the erect penis, usually at night. Sometimes this is accompanied by a sexual dream.

NUCLEUS: See *CELL NUCLEUS.*

O

ORAL SEX: "Eating out," "blow job." Both male and female. One partner puts his or her mouth on the sex organs of the other partner.

ORGANISM: Something that is living.

ORGASM: As sexual feelings grow stronger and stronger, they reaches a peak, and then there is a strong and very pleasurable release. This release is an orgasm. For the male, this release usually comes at the same time as the ejaculation of sperm and semen (the fluid that carries it) from the penis. Both men and women experience this build-up and release throughout their bodies. But the release of tension is especially apparent in the sexual organs; for the man, the penis, for the woman, the clitoris, vagina and uterus. Usually, intense feelings of pleasure and relaxation, centering in the sexual organs, accompany the release. For the male, orgasm usually happens at the same time as ejaculation.

OVA: The eggs stored in a womans' ovaries. The singular term is ovum.

OVARIES: Part of the female reproductive system. The ovaries are two small organs at the end of the fallopian tubes, where the eggs or ova are stored.

OVULATION: Process of ripening and releasing eggs from the ovaries in the female's body.

P

PAD: Also called "sanitary napkin." Used during menstruation to catch and absorb the fluid sloughed off by the uterus.

PAP SMEAR: a testing procedure to check the health of the female cervix. Cancer of the cervix and uterus may be detected in this way to give warning of problems years before they occur.

PELVIC AREA: The area between the pelvic bones below the waist. The area contains several organs, including the male and female reproductive organs.

PELVIC INFLAMMATORY DISEASE (PID): A sexually transmitted disease; can be cured.

PENIS: The male sexual organ.

PERIOD: See *MENSTRUATION.*

PETTING: This is sexual touching below the neck. It usually refers to touching the breasts or penis or vagina, often under the clothing. People usually do this only in private.

PILL: A shortened version of the term "birth control pill." This is an oral contraceptive, made up of various hormone compounds in pill form, used in a specific sequence to prevent ovulation and conception in the woman.

PITUITARY GLAND: Located in the brain. It helps to control the development and functions of the body.

PLACENTA: The organ that develops in the uterus during pregnancy, lining the uterine wall and surrounding the fetus, to which it is attached by the umbilical cord. The placenta helps to nourish the baby and filter the baby's waste into the mother's bloodstream for expulsion. Following the birth of the baby, the placenta is expelled. It is also known as "afterbirth."

"POP THE CHERRY": A slang term for breaking a woman's hymen or maidenhead the first time she has intercourse. Because a small amount of bleeding may occur, the opening of the vagina may appear red like a cherry.

POSITIVE TEST: A blood test result, indicating the presence of an infection or virus.

PREGNANCY TEST: A test given by a doctor or at a laboratory to determine if a woman is pregnant. There are also home kits for this test, which may be purchased at most pharmacies and supermarkets. The home kits are not as reliable.

PREGNANT: A woman is said to be pregnant when she has a fertilized egg that is developing into a baby inside her uterus.

PREGNANT VIRGIN: A female who becomes pregnant but has not engaged in sexual intercourse. Probably the sperm was deposited at the opening of the vagina and found its way inside the vagina.

PREMATURE BABY: A baby that is born before the normal gestation period of forty weeks. A "premmie" can be born as early as five or six months into the pregnancy and survive, thanks to recent medical developments. Usually babies that are born at around seven to eight months into gestation have an excellent chance of survival.

PRENATAL: Term used for the care a woman receives before her baby is born.

PRIVATE PARTS: breasts, reproductive organs, usually buttocks.

PROPHYLACTIC: See *CONDOM.*

PROSTATE: A gland found in men composed of muscular and glandular tissue that surrounds the urethra at the bladder.

PROSTITUTE: A person, male or female, who offers sexual intercourse in exchange for money.

PUBERTY: A time of rapid growth from about twelve to sixteen years of age. Many physical and emotional changes happen at this time.

R

RECESSIVE GENE: A gene passed on from parents to child. If a dominant gene is passed, the child will inherit the dominant gene's trait.

If two recessive genes are passed, the child will inherit the recessive gene's trait.

RECTUM: The lowest part of the large intestine ending in the anus. The solid waste or bowel movements are discharged from the body through this tube.

RHYTHM METHOD: A method of spacing intercourse to avoid the time each month when a woman is most likely to become pregnant. It is not very reliable.

RUBBER: Slang for condom. See *CONDOM.*

S

SCABIES: Tiny mites that infest toe skin, causing itching. May be transmitted sexually, but is also caught in other ways. It is curable.

SCORE: Slang for having intercourse.

SEX DRIVE: Powerful feelings and body sensations that are brought about through sexual attraction.

SEXUAL INTERCOURSE: Having sex, "going all the way," "fucking." The penis is placed inside the vagina. Sperm and semen may be released inside the vagina.

SEXUALLY TRANSMITTED DISEASE: STD, VD. Diseases that are caught through sexual activity, usually intercourse. There are a number of these. Some may be cured, some are either chronic or fatal.

SHAFT (of penis): The area in back of the tip of the penis.

SICKLE CELL ANEMIA: A blood disease or birth defect, usually found in African-Americans.

SPANISH FLY: An aphrodisiac made from Spanish flies that may work by irritating the tube inside the penis, causing an erection. It can harm the sensitive lining of this tube.

SPERM: The zygote found in a male that can fertilize an egg to create a baby. Most men produce billions of sperm in their lifetimes.

SPERM COUNT: A measure used to evaluate the number of sperm in a man's ejaculation. This test is performed in a laboratory.

SPONGE: A method of birth control where sponge-like material is placed inside the female's vagina to cover the cervix.

SPOTTING: A small bloody discharge in women; often between her menstrual period.

STERILIZATION: A medical procedure for ending a man's or woman's ability to have children.

SUDDEN INFANT DEATH SYNDROME. Also known as SIDS, this is the sudden death of a young baby when it stops breathing for no apparent reason. Doctors are not sure why this happens, but think that the baby's breathing control centers in the brain are not fully developed. Babies who go for a long time—more than 20 seconds— between breaths, especially when they are asleep, may be at higher risk. Doctors often place breathing monitors on them that alert the parents if the baby stops breathing for too long. Another term for SIDS is "crib death."

SYPHILIS: A sexually-transmitted disease; can be cured.

T

TAMPON: A cylindrical piece of absorbent material used to catch the menstrual drip. It is inserted into the vagina and should be changed every three to four hours.

TESTICLES: Also called "nuts," "balls." Two male organs contained in the scrotum or sac. They are in back of the penis. Their function is the development of sperm.

TITS: Derogatory slang term for a woman's breasts. See *BREASTS.*

TRAIT: Characteristic such as eye color, skin color. A trait is passed from parents to child by way of genes contained in the sperm and egg.

TRICHOMONIASIS: A sexually-transmitted disease. The symptoms include a discharge that may itch. May also be caught from a public bath.

TUBAL LIGATION: A form of permanent birth control whereby a woman's fallopian tubes are cut and cauterized.

TWINS: Two babies grown at the same time in the uterus, usually born about the same time. Identical twins are babies grown from the same egg and sperm. Fraternal twins are babies who are born at the same time, but were developed from different eggs and sperm. Siamese twins are identical twins that are attached at birth. These twins are separated if possible.

U

ULCERS: Sores on or in the body.

UMBILICAL CORD: A tube approximately three feet in length which connects the unborn baby to its mother in the uterus. The baby receives its nourishment and oxygen and releases its waste through the cord.

URETHRA: The tube for releasing liquid waste, or urine.

URINE: Liquid waste released from the body through the penis in the male, through the urethral tube and opening in the female.

UTERUS: The female organ where the baby develops from a fertilized egg.

V

VAGINA: Female sex organ. It is a tube about five inches long with an opening between the legs. Menstrual drip is released through it and it is also the birth canal by which a baby is born.

VAGINAL DISCHARGE: Normal white or colorless fluid leaked out of the vagina. If it has a strong odor and color, it may be an indication of an infection and should be treated at the clinic or by a doctor as soon as possible.

VAGINITIS: General term for several infections of the vagina. A sexually transmitted disease, it may be cured.

VAS DEFERENS: The tube that carries sperm from the testes to the penis.

VASECTOMY: The male form of sterilization. The tubes by which the sperm travels through the penis are cut and cauterized so that sperm is not released but reabsorbed back into the body.

VENEREAL DISEASE: See *SEXUALLY TRANSMITTED DISEASES.*

VENEREAL WARTS: Small lumps caused by a virus, a sexually transmitted disease. Can be spread by body fluids as well. Appear around the sexual organs and anus. Can be cured.

VIRGIN: Someone who has never had sexual intercourse. This term applies to both men and women.

VITAL ORGANS: Parts of the body needed for survival such as the heart, liver and kidneys.

W

WET DREAM: See *NOCTURNAL EMISSIONS.*

WITHDRAWAL: Stopping intercourse, pulling the penis out of the vagina before ejaculation. This is not a very good method of birth control.

Y

YEAST INFECTIONS: A common infection experienced by most women. Can be treated by a doctor and over-the-counter applications are also available. May be sexually transmitted.

APPENDIX I
DISTRIBUTION FOR TOTAL NUMBER OF QUESTIONS

Grade	Human Heredity	Physical	Pregnancy and Birth	Conception Control	Venereal Diseases	Relationships and Behavior	Total
Lower Elementary	5	66	60	4	3	4	172
Special Education	2	34	39	4	7	46	130
Upper Elementary	32	153	131	24	11	81	432
7th Grade	37	90	91	27	19	59	323
8th Grade	14	66	53	32	76	111	352
9th Grade	8	45	92	65	69	155	452
10th Grade	7	50	105	86	128	196	523
Total	105	504	571	242	313	652	2434

APPENDIX II
SOURCES OF INFORMATION ON SEXUALITY

School nurse, counsellor or science teacher.
Local Planned Parenthood Council
City or County Sexually Transmitted Disease (Venereal Disease) Clinic.
Local Child Abuse Council.
Local Police Department (on sex and the law).
Local Probate Court officials.
Your doctor or nurse.
Popular Science magazine.
Newspapers.
   Television programs, especially ones on Public Broadcasting System (PBS) stations.
Textbooks on human sexuality.

FURTHER READINGS

Bell. *Changing Bodies, Changing Lives.* New York: Random House, 1980.

Boston Women's Health Book Collective. *Our Bodies Ourselves.* New York: Simon and Schuster, 1976.

Calderone, M. and E. Johnson. *Family Book of Sexuality,* New York: Bantam Books, 1983.

Diagram Group. *Man's Body: An Owner's Manual.* Paddington Press, 1976.

Diagram Group. *Woman's Body.* Paddington Press, 1976.

Gordon, S. *You Would If You Loved Me,* New York: Ed-U–Press.

Gordon, S. and J. Gordon. *Did the Sun Shine Before You Were Born?* Third World Press, 1977.

Gordon, Sol. *Facts About Sex for Today's Youth,* John Day Company, 1973.

Guttmacher, Alan, Institute. *Teenage Pregnancy: The Problem That Hasn't Gone Away,* New York, 1981.

Kelly, G. *Learning About Sex.* New York: Barron's Educational Series, Inc., 1976.

Kelly, G.P. *Sexuality: The Human Perspective.* New York: Barron's Educational Series, 1980.

Life Educational Reprints Program, Box 834, Radio City Post Office, New York, 10019.

Mayle, P. *Where Did I Come From?* New York, Lyle Stuart, 1973.

McWhirter, N. *Guinness Book of World Records,* New York: Bantam Books, 1990.

National Clearinghouse for Family Planning Information, Public Health Service, Health Services Administration, Office of Family Planning, P.O. box 2225, Rockville, Maryland 20852. A catalog, "Family Planning Materials."

INDEX